Mac® OS X and Office v.X
Keyboard Shortcuts

Guy Hart-Davis

McGraw-Hill/Osborne
New York Chicago San Francisco
Lisbon London Madrid Mexico City
Milan New Delhi San Juan
Seoul Singapore Sydney Toronto

The McGraw·Hill Companies

McGraw-Hill/Osborne
2100 Powell Street, 10th Floor
Emeryville, California 94608
U.S.A.

To arrange bulk purchase discounts for sales promotions, premiums, or fund-raisers, please contact **McGraw-Hill**/Osborne at the above address. For information on translations or book distributors outside the U.S.A., please see the International Contact Information page immediately following the index of this book.

Mac® OS X and Office v.X Keyboard Shortcuts

1234567890 DOC DOC 01987654

ISBN 0-07-225501-3

Publisher	**Copy Editor**
Brandon A. Nordin	Judith Brown
Vice President &	**Proofreader**
Associate Publisher	Paul Medoff
Scott Rogers	**Indexer**
Editorial Director	Claire Splan
Roger Stewart	**Composition**
Project Editor	Tara A. Davis, Dick Schwartz
Jenn Tust	**Illustrators**
Acquisitions Coordinator	Kathleen Edwards, Melinda Lytle
Agatha Kim	**Series Design**
Technical Editor	Dick Schwartz, Peter Hancik
Bill Bruns	

This book was composed with Corel VENTURA™ Publisher.

Contents

Introduction

Need to get your work done quickly and accurately with Mac OS X and Office v.X? Then use the keyboard more.

Mac OS X is a superb and beautiful graphical operating system, and the mouse is great for precise graphical operations, but for invoking commands quickly and accurately, the keyboard rules. This book shows you how to make the most of your keyboard by using the keyboard shortcuts built into Mac OS X and Office v.X—and by creating your own keyboard shortcuts to supplement those built in.

Who Is This Book For?

This book is for users of Mac OS X and Office v.X who want to get their work done more quickly, accurately, and efficiently. That probably means *you*. Unless you find yourself spending large chunks of your workday staring into space or drumming your fingers to the latest beats while waiting for more work to show up, you can benefit from saving time and effort by using keyboard shortcuts.

This book assumes that you're familiar with the basics of the applications you're using, and that you want to use them more efficiently. For example, this book assumes that you know how to start Mac OS X, log on and off, run applications, use the Finder, and perform basic file management. Similarly, this book doesn't tell you what a Word document or an Excel worksheet *is*, but rather how to create and work in documents and worksheets faster and more efficiently.

What Does This Book Cover?

This book explains how to use keyboard shortcuts in Mac OS X and the Office v.X applications: Word, Excel, PowerPoint, and Entourage. Coverage is arranged by application and by topic. Within each topic, you'll learn the keyboard shortcuts you need to perform essential actions swiftly without reaching for your mouse.

Besides telling you how to use, customize, and create keyboard shortcuts, this book also tells you how to choose the best keyboard for your needs and your budget and how to configure it. Some Mac keyboards work well for many people, but Apple is notorious for putting style over substance in this area as in many others—for example, PowerBooks still have no dedicated [Page Up], [Page Down], [Home], and [End] keys, just as they still have no right mouse button, even though there's plenty of space for both these missing features.

So you might be able to benefit from upgrading your keyboard if you haven't done so already. (You can even upgrade the keyboard on a PowerBook.) This book explains the range of keyboards available, from conventional keyboards to one-handed keyboards and keyless keyboards, and it explains how to configure your keyboard for comfort and speed. The trinity of keyboard, mouse, and monitor largely govern how comfortable your computer use is—and there's no sense in being less comfortable than you need to be, even if you're not yet suffering from RSI.

Conventions Used in This Book

This book uses the following conventions to make the text easy to follow:

- Key caps such as [⌘]-[Option]-[Escape] represent keyboard shortcuts. Hyphens mean that you should press the keys in combination.

- The | symbol represents making a choice from a menu. For example, "choose File | Print" means that you should open the File menu and choose the Print command from it. (Usually, you'll press [⌘]-[P] instead, because it's quicker.)

- The symbol represents the menu (the one that appears at the left end of the menu bar).

Keyboard Basics—and How to Enhance Your Keyboard

You'd be hard put to find a Mac user who doesn't know what a keyboard is—but it would probably be nearly as difficult to find a Mac user who uses the keyboard to the max. This chapter shows you how to configure your keyboard as well as possible and use such accessibility options as may help you. The chapter starts by making sure you know your way around your keyboard and the correct way to press keyboard shortcuts. After all, there's no point in getting the basics wrong.

>> Note: *You might also benefit from upgrading to a better keyboard. The appendix discusses the different types of keyboards available and suggests how to choose among them.*

Understanding the Standard Keys

Most keyboards for desktop Macs contain between 101 and 115 keys that break down as follows. Figure 1-1 shows an example of a fairly typical Mac keyboard.

- Twenty-six letter keys for the letters a through z.
- A [Spacebar] to put spaces between characters.
- Two sets of keys for the single-digit numbers (0 through 9), one set appearing as a row above the letter keys and one set on the numeric keypad. The keys in the row of number keys double as symbol keys.
- Fifteen to 18 keys for mainstream punctuation symbols (for example, comma, period, and semicolon) and other symbols (for example, + and ~). The numeric keypad typically includes symbols used for basic mathematical operations (+ for addition, – for subtraction, / for division, and * for multiplication) and a period for a decimal place.

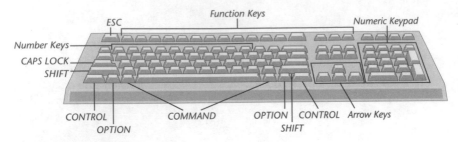

Figure 1-1 *A fairly typical Mac keyboard layout*

- A ⟨Tab⟩ key for entering tabs and for navigating from one interface element to another.
- Two ⟨Return⟩ keys for entering carriage returns and "clicking" the selected button in dialog boxes.
- Two ⟨Shift⟩ keys to change the case of the key pressed, and a ⟨Caps Lock⟩ key to lock the letter keys in the capital position.
- Six modifier keys: two ⟨Ctrl⟩ or ⟨Control⟩ keys, two ⟨Alt⟩/⟨Option⟩ keys, and two ⟨⌘⟩ keys (discussed in the next section).
- A ⟨Delete Forward⟩ key for deleting the selection or the character after the insertion point, and a ⟨Delete⟩ key for deleting the character before the insertion point.
- Eight or more navigation keys: four arrow keys ⟨←⟩, ⟨→⟩, ⟨↑⟩, and ⟨↓⟩; a ⟨Home⟩ key for moving to the beginning of an item; an ⟨End⟩ key for moving to the end of an item; a ⟨Page Up⟩ key for moving up by a "page" of information; and a ⟨Page Down⟩ key for moving down by a page.
- Twelve or more function keys, numbered ⟨F1⟩ to ⟨F12⟩ or the appropriate higher number, for invoking functionality built into the operating system and into applications. Some keyboards have 16 function keys.
- An ⟨Esc⟩ key for canceling an action or "clicking" the Cancel button in a dialog box.

Some keyboards have extra keys for increasing and decreasing the playback volume, for toggling muting of all sound, and for ejecting the selected CD or other medium.

Using the Modifier Keys

The standard keys discussed in the previous section are mostly easy enough to use: to get an *a*, you press ⟨A⟩; to get a 1, you press ⟨1⟩; and so on. To use a keyboard shortcut, you typically press one or more of the *modifier keys*—keys that modify the effect of the key you press—with another key. (That sentence says "typically" because some keyboard shortcuts don't use any modifier key, as you'll see later in this book.)

Standard keyboards for Macs include four modifier keys (Figure 1-2):

- Shift This key derives from the typewriter and changes the case of the letter. The name comes from the Shift key on a typewriter physically shifting the typewriter mechanism—either lifting the platen or lowering the typebars so that the top part of the typebar (which contains the uppercase letter) strikes the platen rather than the lower part of the typebar (which contains the lowercase letter). (*Typebars* are the metal bars containing the letters. The *platen* is the roller around which the sheet of paper is wrapped and fed, and against which the typebars strike.)

- ⌘ This key (the Command key, which also shows the Apple logo) is used in Mac OS X to trigger keyboard shortcuts. For example, to issue a Print command in many applications, you can press ⌘-P. Mac OS X uses many ⌘-Shift shortcuts. For example, pressing ⌘-Shift-A with the Finder active displays your Applications folder.

- Alt/Option The Alt/Option key alters the keypress.

>> **Note:** *This book refers to the* Alt/Option *key as* Option *from here on.*

- Control This key (often marked Ctrl) is used both to trigger keyboard shortcuts and to produce a right click with a single-button mouse (you hold down Control while you click).

⌘, Control, Option, and Shift can be used in combination, thus producing many more key combinations—for example, ⌘-M, ⌘-Option-M, ⌘-Option-Shift-M, ⌘-Shift-M, Option-M, and Option-Shift-M. The more keys in a combination, the harder it is for most users to press, but the less chance that any user will press that combination by accident.

PowerBooks and iBooks include another modifier key on their keyboard: the function Fn key, which is typically used to provide additional functionality on a keyboard that doesn't have enough keys for each separate function.

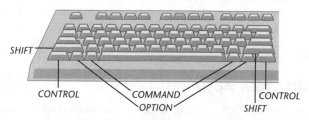

Figure 1-2 *Desktop Mac keyboards have four modifier keys:* ⌘ *,* Shift *,* Option *, and* Control.

For example, on current PowerBook models, you must press (Fn) and the function key to invoke the function key, because the key's primary mapping is to a hardware function: on G4 PowerBooks, the (F1) key without (Fn) pressed decreases the screen's brightness, the (F2) key without (Fn) pressed increases the brightness, the (F3) key without (Fn) pressed mutes the sound, and so on.

PowerBooks and iBooks also have an embedded keypad to provide the functionality of the keypad on a full-size keyboard. The embedded keypad appears on the right-hand side of the keyboard, with the letter (J) doubling for (1), (K) for (2), and (L) for (3). You press (NumLock) to activate the keypad function.

Pressing Key Combinations

To use a key combination, you typically hold down the modifier key or keys while you press the alphanumeric key or other key. For example, to issue a Print command, you press (⌘) and hold it down, press and release (P), and then release (⌘). To press (⌘)-(Shift)-(A), you press and hold down (⌘) and (Shift) together while you press (A).

》 Note: *If you're familiar with Windows, you'll know that Windows lets you display a menu in the active application by pressing (Alt) followed by the underlined letter in the menu's name. For example, to display the File menu, you press (F). This letter is called the* access key *or* mnemonic. *Mac OS X doesn't use access keys, but you can use the menus via the keyboard by using Full Keyboard Access. See "Using Full Keyboard Access" in Chapter 2 for details.*

Configuring Your Keyboard

Mac OS X ships with default keyboard settings that work tolerably well for many people. But to get the best results from your keyboard, you may need to configure it.

Mac OS X supports three different types of configuration settings:

- **Basic keyboard settings**   You can configure the speed and delay for repeating characters, and the speed at which the cursor (the insertion point) blinks. If you have a PowerBook with an illuminated keyboard, you can specify when to use the illumination.

- **Keyboard layouts**   You can change the logical layout of your physical keyboard to one of a number of alternative layouts.

- **Universal Access features**   You can use special accessibility features that Mac OS X offers to make your keyboard easier to use.

》 Note: *If these three types of configuration settings don't give you the results you need, you may want to get a different keyboard. I'll discuss your options in the appendix.*

Changing Basic Keyboard Settings

Your first option is to change the rate at which the cursor blinks and the rate at which Mac OS X repeats characters when you keep a key pressed down. To configure these options, choose | System Preferences to display the System Preferences window, and then click the Keyboard & Mouse icon to display the Keyboard & Mouse sheet. If necessary, click the Keyboard tab to display its contents (Figure 1-3).

Drag the Key Repeat Rate slider and the Delay Until Repeat slider to suitable positions. Type in the Type Here To Test Settings box to make sure the resulting repeat rate works for you.

Press ⌘-Q or choose System Preferences | Quit System Preferences to close System Preferences.

Using the Keyboard Universal Access Features

If you find it difficult to press keys or key combinations consistently, you may be able to improve matters by using Mac OS X's Universal Access features. These features are designed to help users who have mild to moderate disabilities, but no disability is required—if you're able bodied, and you find an accessibility feature useful, go ahead and use it. It's not like parking in a Disabled space.

There are two main Universal Access features for the keyboard:

- Sticky Keys enables you to "stick" the modifier keys on so that you can press them one at a time (for example, ⌘, then Shift, then A) instead of having to press them all together.

- Slow Keys lets you tell Mac OS X to wait a moment before accepting a keypress, and to play a sound confirming the keypress. Slow Keys is good if you find yourself triggering keys accidentally by pressing them while trying to press another key.

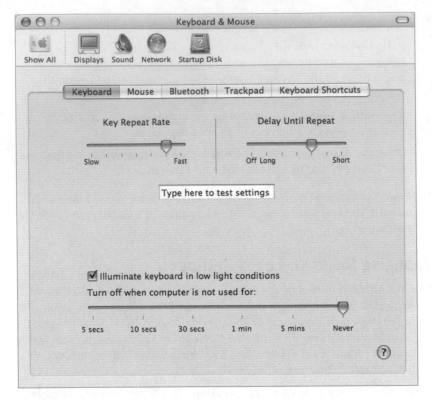

Figure 1-3 *You can change your keyboard's repeat rate and delay on the Keyboard tab of the Keyboard & Mouse sheet in System Preferences.*

To configure the Universal Access features for the keyboard, follow these steps:

1. Choose | System Preferences to display the System Preferences window.

2. Click the Universal Access icon in the System area to display the Universal Access sheet.

3. Click the Keyboard tab button to display the tab's contents (Figure 1-4).

4. In the For Difficulties Pressing More Than One Key At A Time area, choose options as appropriate:

   - Select the On option button in the Sticky Keys area to turn on Sticky Keys.

   - Select the Press The Shift Key Five Times To Turn Sticky Keys On Or Off check box if you want to be able to turn Sticky Keys on and off from the keyboard.

   - Select the Beep When A Modifier Key Is Set check box if you want Mac OS X to play a sound when you press a modifier key.

- Select the Display Pressed Keys On Screen check box if you want Mac OS X to display symbols on screen for the modifier keys that you've pressed so far:

5. In the For Difficulties With Initial Or Repeated Keystrokes area, choose options as appropriate:

   - Select the On option button in the Slow Keys area to turn on Slow Keys.
   - Select the Use Click Key Sounds check box if you want Mac OS X to play a click sound to confirm each key you press. (The effect of this sound is a bit like using a typewriter.)
   - Drag the Acceptance Delay slider to a suitable setting.

6. Press ⌘-Q or choose System Preferences | Quit System Preferences to close System Preferences.

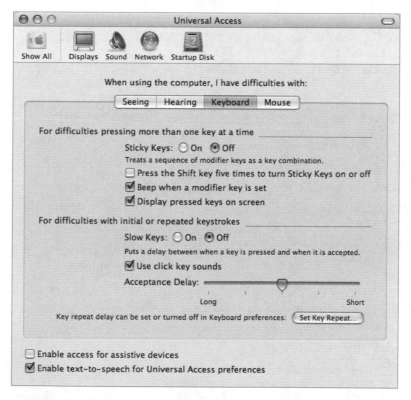

Figure 1-4 *Mac OS X's Universal Access features can make your keyboard easier to use.*

Using Mouse Keys

If you want to use your keyboard as much as possible, another accessibility option to try is Mouse Keys, which lets you control the mouse by using the arrow keys on your keyboard. Using Mouse Keys doesn't suit everybody: some people find them too slow and clumsy, but it might be worth finding out for yourself.

To turn on MouseKeys, follow these steps:

1. Choose ⬢ | System Preferences to display the System Preferences window.
2. Click the Universal Access icon in the System area to display the Universal Access sheet.
3. Click the Mouse tab button to display the tab's contents (Figure 1-5).
4. Select the On option button in the Mouse Keys area to turn Mouse Keys on.
5. If you want to be able to turn Mouse Keys on quickly using the keyboard, select the Press The Option Key Five Times To Turn Mouse Keys On Or Off check box.

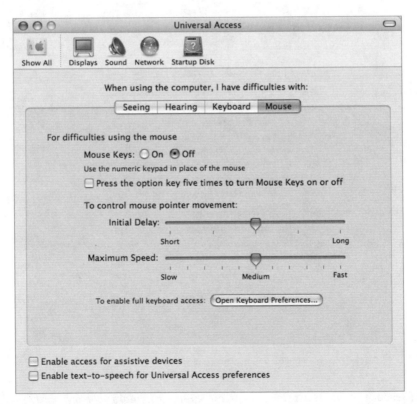

Figure 1-5 *Mac OS X's Mouse Keys feature lets you control the mouse by using the arrow keys on your keyboard.*

6. Adjust the Initial Delay slider to control how quickly Mouse Keys kicks in when you press ⬅, ➡, ⬆, or ⬇ on the numeric keypad.

7. Adjust the Maximum Speed slider to control the maximum speed at which Mouse Keys moves the mouse pointer when you're pressing ⬅, ➡, ⬆, or ⬇. (Mouse Keys moves the mouse pointer slowly at first, then speeds it up to the maximum speed if you keep pressing the key.)

8. Press ⌘-Q or choose System Preferences | Quit System Preferences to close System Preferences.

Using Alternative Keyboard Layouts

The standard layout of keys on a keyboard, as you'll know from glancing at your keyboard every day, has the letters QWERTYUIOP across the top row and is generally known by the acronym QWERTY. The QWERTY layout is used almost universally in the English-typing world but isn't the most efficient or comfortable layout for extended typing.

QWERTY was designed in the 1870s by Christopher Latham Sholes, the leading inventor of the first typewriter produced in commercial quantities. The prime consideration influencing the layout was the need to prevent the keybars from jamming when the user was typing fast, but commercial considerations were also involved: Sholes included all the letters for the word *typewriter* in the top line so that his salesmen could type it more easily when demonstrating the typewriter. The result was that only about 36 percent of the letters you type on a QWERTY keyboard are on the home row, so your fingers have to move frequently to the other rows of keys.

As you'll probably agree from your experience of learning to type, the QWERTY layout isn't easy to learn; if you use it extensively, you may also agree that it's not efficient to use either. But because it became the standard layout relatively quickly after its introduction, and because it has remained the standard layout in the English-typing world, QWERTY has such a lock on the market that no alternative keyboard layout has gained much traction. Not surprisingly, few people want to learn to type again, and QWERTY works well enough once you've learned it, so it seems likely to be with us to stay.

The keyboard layout is hard-coded into a typewriter, so to change the letter that a key delivered, you'd need to saw the keybar off and weld on a different one. With computers, making changes is much easier. The physical layout of the keyboard is hard-coded, although with some keyboards, you can pop off the key caps (the caps that constitute the physical keys) and slide them back on in different places if you choose. (This works only for standard keyboards and invalidates most warranties you might care to mention.) But the logical layout can be changed either on the keyboard or on the computer with minimal effort. Should you want to try a different keyboard layout, you need only tell your keyboard or your computer so.

Which Layout Should You Use?

At this point, you're probably not too excited about the possibilities of logical layouts unless you have a particular logical layout in mind. After all, to use a different layout, you either need to buy a keyboard that has that layout, physically customize your keyboard to show that layout (for example, by rearranging the key caps or pasting stickers over the letters on them), or touch-type on a keyboard whose keys show different letters than they deliver. (You should be touch-typing in any case, because doing so saves you a huge amount of time and effort over looking for the keys. But even so, having each key produce a different letter than it bears can be disconcerting, especially when you're trying to type passwords and can't see on screen which letters you're getting.)

For most people, the primary alternative is one of the implementations of the Dvorak keyboard layout—for example, the Dvorak layout that comes built into Mac OS X. Unlike QWERTY, the Dvorak layout was designed for efficient typing in English, and in typical use, about 74 percent of keystrokes are on the home row, so your fingers needn't move nearly as far as with QWERTY. August Dvorak, the inventor of the Dvorak layout, also laid out the keys to use as much as possible the hand's natural drumming rhythm from pinkie to index finger, which helps make the typing motion faster and more comfortable.

The Dvorak layout has many enthusiasts (full disclosure: I'm one) but has barely scratched the surface of the mainstream typing market because QWERTY, as the default keyboard format, has the market pretty thoroughly sewn up. You can buy keyboards with Dvorak layouts from specialist keyboard retailers, but the easiest way to get started is to download a Dvorak key chart from the Internet, apply the Dvorak keyboard layout (using the technique discussed next), and learn to touch-type with it.

Dvorak's far from the only option: Mac OS X supports an impressive array of different keyboard layouts. But unless you learned to type on a particular keyboard layout, or a layout offers better key placement for particular keys you find difficult to press, you won't usually have a strong reason for choosing it over your existing keyboard layout.

>> **Note:** *You can add keyboard layouts to those that Mac OS X provides by copying the keyboard layout file to your Mac. Put the file in /Library (your Mac's main Library folder) to make it available for every user. Put the file in your ~/Library folder (the Library folder in your Home folder) to keep it to yourself.*

Applying a Different Keyboard Layout

To apply a different keyboard layout, follow these steps:

   1. Choose | System Preferences to display the System Preferences window.

2. Click the International icon in the Personal area to display the International sheet.

3. Click the Input Menu tab button to display the Input Menu tab (Figure 1-6).

4. Select the check box in the On column for each keyboard layout you want to add to the input menu. If you just want to have one layout available, make sure that its check box is the only one selected.

5. If you choose to load two or more layouts, and you want to be able to switch among them by using the mouse, make sure the Show Input Menu In Menu Bar check box is selected.

6. If you choose to load two or more layouts, and you want to be able to switch among them by using the keyboard rather than the input menu, click the Options button to display the Input Menu Shortcuts pane (shown at the top of the next page). Make sure the Holding Down Command+Option And Typing Space Will Step Through All Items In The Input Menu check box is selected, and then click the OK button.

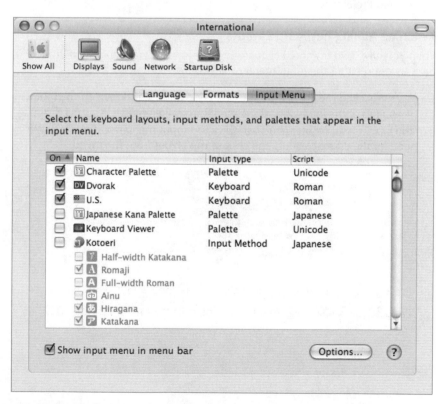

Figure 1-6 *Use the Input Menu tab of the International sheet in System Preferences to apply a different logical keyboard layout.*

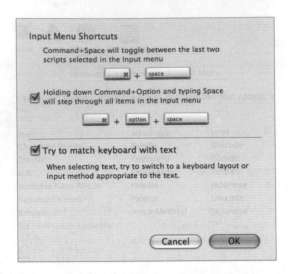

7. Press ⌘-Q or choose System Preferences | Quit System Preferences to close System Preferences.

Switching Among Keyboard Layouts

When you have two or more keyboard layouts loaded, you can switch among them by using either the input menu or keyboard shortcuts:

- If you selected the Show Input Menu In Menu Bar check box on the Input Menu tab of the International sheet in System Preferences, Mac OS X displays the input menu on the menu bar. Click the input menu icon (which shows an icon for the current layout) and choose the layout from the menu:

- Press ⌘-Spacebar to toggle between the last two layouts you've used.
- Press ⌘-Option-Spacebar to select the next item in the input menu.

2

Mac OS X Keyboard Shortcuts

Since its beginning, Mac OS has had the reputation of being the graphical operating system to end all graphical operating systems—and indeed most Mac users perform an even higher proportion of their daily work with the mouse than do most Windows users. But Mac OS X supports a staggering number of keyboard shortcuts that enable you to take a wide variety of actions without removing your hands from the keys.

This chapter shows you how to make the most of Mac OS X's keyboard shortcuts. You'll also learn how to use modifier keys with the mouse to modify the mouse's actions.

Standard Mac OS X Keyboard Shortcuts

Mac OS X includes various keyboard shortcuts that work in the Finder (including on the desktop) and in most applications. These shortcuts encompass undoing and redoing actions; opening, closing, saving, and printing files; working with text; cutting, copying, and pasting; and getting information about an object or help with a topic.

Shortcuts for Undoing and Redoing Actions

Control-Z

Undo the previous action

Mac OS X enables you to undo most actions you can take. But be warned that you can't undo emptying the Trash.

⌘-Shift-Z

Redo the previous undone action

Press this shortcut to redo an action you've just undone.

Shortcuts for Opening, Closing, Saving, and Printing Files

⌘-O

Display the Open dialog box

⌘-W

Close the active file

If the active file contains unsaved changes, the application prompts you to save them.

⌘-S

Save the active file

If the active file has never been saved, the application displays the Save sheet so that you can specify the folder and the filename. If the file has been saved before, the application saves the file without displaying the Save sheet.

⌘-P

Display the Print dialog box

Using Keyboard Shortcuts in Common Dialog Boxes and Sheets

After displaying a common dialog box (such as the Open dialog box) or a common sheet (such as the Save sheet, which you'll also hear referred to as the "Save dialog box"), you can use keyboard shortcuts to work in it.

≫ Note: *What most people call the Save dialog box is technically a sheet that stays attached to its document. Whereas most dialog boxes prevent you from taking further actions in the application until you dismiss the dialog box, Save sheets prevent you from taking action in the document to which the Save sheet is attached. However, you can switch to other documents open in the same application and work in them if necessary while the Save sheet is open in the first document.*

Shortcuts for Working with Common Dialog Boxes and Sheets

Return

Click the default button

The default button is the button that has the blue focus when the dialog box or sheet is displayed. For example, the default button in the Open dialog box is the Open button, and the default button in the Save sheet is the Save button.

Esc, **⌘**-**.**
Click the Cancel button

Pressing one of these shortcuts closes the dialog box or sheet.

⌘-**D**
Select the desktop

⌘-**Shift**-**H**
Select your Home folder

⌘-**Shift**-**C**
Select your computer

⌘-**Shift**-**A**
Select your Applications folder

⌘-**Shift**-**I**
Select your iDisk

Shortcuts for Working with Message Boxes

You can use the following keyboard shortcuts for clicking the buttons in message boxes that use the Yes, No, and Cancel buttons (or a subset of them).

Y
Click the Yes button

N
Click the No button

C
Click the Cancel button

Working with Text

Mac OS X and most applications support the following keyboard shortcuts for working with text.

Shortcuts for Deleting Text

[Delete]

Delete one character to the left of the insertion point

[Option]-[Delete]

Delete one word to the left of the insertion point

If the insertion point is in a word rather than between words, [Option]-[Delete] deletes to the beginning of that word.

[Forward Delete], [Fn]-[Delete]

Delete one character to the right of the insertion point

If your keyboard doesn't have a [Forward Delete] key, press [Fn]-[Delete] instead.

[Option]-[Forward Delete], [⌘]-[Fn]-[Delete]

Delete one word to the right of the insertion point

If the insertion point is in a word rather than between words, these shortcuts delete to the end of the word.

Shortcuts for Moving Around in Text

[←]

Move one character to the left

[→]

Move one character to the right

[↑]

Move up one line

[↓]

Move down one line

⌘-←

Move to the start of the line

⌘-→

Move to the end of the line

⌘-↑

Move to the start of the document

⌘-↓

Move to the end of the document

Option-←

Move one word to the left

Option-→

Move one word to the right

Option-↑

Move to the beginning of the current paragraph or preceding paragraph

If the insertion point is in a paragraph, pressing this shortcut moves the insertion point to the beginning of the paragraph. If the insertion point is already at the beginning of a paragraph, pressing this shortcut moves the insertion point to the beginning of the previous paragraph.

Option-↓

Move to the end of the current paragraph or next paragraph

If the insertion point is in a paragraph, pressing this shortcut moves the insertion point to the end of the paragraph. If the insertion point is already at the end of a paragraph, pressing this shortcut moves the insertion point to the end of the next paragraph.

Shortcuts for Selecting Text and Objects

Shift-→

Select the next character to the right

Mac OS X, Finder, and Safari

Shift - ←

Select the next character to the left

Option - Shift - →

Select to the end of the current word or next word

If the insertion point is in a word, pressing Option - Shift - → selects to the end of that word. If the insertion point is between words, pressing this shortcut selects to the end of the next word.

Option - Shift - ←

Select to the beginning of the current word or previous word

If the insertion point is in a word, pressing Option - Shift - ← selects to the start of that word. If the insertion point is between words, pressing this shortcut selects to the start of the previous word.

Shift - ↑

Select one line up

Shift - ↓

Select one line down

⌘ - A

Select all the contents of the current object

Shortcuts for Formatting Text

Mac OS X and most applications support the following keyboard shortcuts for applying basic formatting to text (and some other objects).

⌘ - B

Toggle boldface

⌘ - I

Toggle italic

⌘ - U

Toggle single underline

-T

Display the Font dialog box

This shortcut works only in some applications.

 -+

Increase the font size

 -−

Decrease the font size

Shortcuts for Checking Spelling

Mac OS X features an integrated Spelling Checker that works with many Cocoa (Mac OS X-native) applications, such as the iLife applications, Mail, and TextEdit. Mac OS X offers two keyboard shortcuts for checking spelling. These shortcuts are most useful if you've turned off the Check Spelling As You Type feature (choose Edit | Spelling | Check Spelling As You Type from an application that supports spell checking).

Start a spelling check

 -;

Check the spelling of the active word

Place the insertion point in the word you want to check, and then press this shortcut.

Cutting, Copying, and Pasting

Cut, Copy, and Paste are basic operations that you can perform in the Finder (for example, copying and moving files or folders) and in many applications. When you make your selections with the keyboard rather than the mouse, issuing the Cut, Copy, and Paste commands from the keyboard is faster and more convenient than using toolbar buttons or menu commands.

Shortcuts for Cut, Copy, and Paste

⌘-X

Cut the selected item

This shortcut either cuts the selected item from the active document (for example, cutting a chart in Excel) or marks the selected files and folders for moving.

Mac OS X, Finder, and Safari

⌘-C

Copy the selected item

This shortcut either copies the selected item (for example, a paragraph of text in Word or an object in PowerPoint) or copies information about the selected file in preparation for pasting.

⌘-V

Paste the current item from the Clipboard

This shortcut pastes the current item at the position of the insertion point (for example, in Word or PowerPoint). With files and folders, it pastes the copied files or folders into the Finder window that contains the focus.

Getting Information and Getting Help

You can use the following keyboard shortcuts to display the Get Info dialog box, which contains information about the selected object.

Shortcuts for Getting Information About an Object

⌘-I

Display the Get Info window

The nature and extent of the information displayed in the Get Info window depends on the object selected: a disk, a document, an alias, multiple objects, and so on.

» Note: *Mac OS X opens a new Get Info window for each separate object for which you press ⌘-I. To display information about a different object in the same Get Info window, use the next shortcut.*

⌘-Option-I

Display information about this object in the existing Get Info window

Shortcuts for Getting Help

You can use the following keyboard shortcut to launch or activate the Help Viewer, in which you can search for help on a specific topic.

⌘-Shift-?

Launch or activate the Help Viewer

Working with Applications and Windows

Mac OS X provides keyboard shortcuts for cycling through, closing, and minimizing windows; switching among the running applications; hiding one or more running applications; managing windows using Exposé; and closing applications either gently or forcibly.

Shortcuts for Cycling Through, Closing, and Minimizing Windows

Cycle forward among the open windows

This shortcut works for the Finder and for all applications that can have multiple windows open. Press ⌘-` as many times as necessary to select each open window in turn until you reach the window you want to work with.

Cycle backward among the open windows

This shortcut works for the Finder and for all applications that can have multiple windows open. Press ⌘-~ (or ⌘-Shift-`, if you prefer to think of it that way) as many times as necessary to select each open window in turn until you reach the window you want to work with.

>> **Note:** *The Finder has a little difference with the* ⌘-` *and* ⌘-~ *shortcuts: it counts the desktop itself as an open window, so one of your keypresses will select the desktop.*

⌘-W

Close the active window

If the window is the last window for the document and contains unsaved changes, the application prompts you to save the changes. Press Return to invoke the Save button from the keyboard. Press ⌘-D to invoke the Don't Save button from the keyboard.

⌘-M

Minimize the active window

⌘-Option-M

Minimize all nonminimized windows in the active application

By minimizing all the windows for the active application, you can see more easily which other applications and windows you have open.

» Caution: ⌘-Option-M *has a different use in Word v.X: it displays the* *Paragraph dialog box.*

Option-click a window's close button

Close all the open windows in that application

If a window is the last window for a document that contains unsaved changes, the application prompts you to save the changes.

⌘-drag

Move a window in the background without bringing it to the foreground

Shortcuts for Switching Among the Running Applications

⌘-Tab

Cycle through the running applications

Press ⌘-Tab repeatedly to highlight each running application on the Dock, from left to right. Stop pressing ⌘-Tab to activate the highlighted application.

» Tip: *Pressing* ⌘-Tab *once selects the previous application, so you can use this* *shortcut to toggle quickly between two applications—you don't need to press* ⌘-Tab *multiple times to cycle through all open applications.*

⌘-Shift-Tab

Cycle through the running applications in reverse order

As for ⌘-Tab, but in reverse order: Mac OS X highlights each running application on the Dock, from right to left. When you stop pressing ⌘-Shift-Tab, Mac OS X activates the currently highlighted application.

Shortcuts for Hiding Running Applications

You can quickly clear your desktop and switch among your running applications without taking your hands off the keyboard.

⌘-H

Hide the active application

Hide the active application so that you can quickly access the other applications you have running.

⌘-Option-H

Hide all other applications except the active application

Hide all other applications so that you can focus on the active application without distraction and clear space on your desktop for it. Use ⌘-Tab to access the application again.

Using Exposé to Manage Windows

If you use the keyboard extensively, chances are that you'll find Exposé one of the most exciting additions to Panther over previous versions of Mac OS X. Exposé lets you quickly shrink your open windows so that you can see which applications you have open and pick the one you want to work with.

Shortcuts for Exposé

F9

Shrink the screen to display all open windows

Click the application you want to use, or press F9 again to return the display to its previous state.

F10

Shrink the screen to display all open windows in the active application

Click the window you want to display, or press F10 again to return the display to its previous state.

F11

Hide all open windows to display the desktop

Press F11 again to return the display to its previous state.

≫ Note: *You can change the keyboard shortcuts used for Exposé by working in the Keyboard section of the Exposé sheet in System Preferences (choose | System Preferences, and then click the Exposé icon). If necessary, you can add modifier keys to the keys listed in the drop-down lists by pressing ⌘, Option, Control, or Shift (or a combination of them) while the drop-down list is open.*

Quitting and Force-Quitting Applications

When an application is working correctly, you close it by quitting it. When an application *hangs* (stops responding), you'll need to *force-quit* it—close it forcibly.

Shortcuts for Quitting and Force-Quitting Applications

⌘-Q

Quit the application

Mac OS X, Finder, and Safari

If any files open in the application contain unsaved changes, the application prompts you to save them.

Option-click an application's Dock icon

Display the shortcut menu with the Force Quit command

When a running application hangs, Option-click its icon on the Dock and issue the Force Quit command from the shortcut menu (shown here). If the application doesn't respond to Option-click, use the Force Quit Applications dialog box instead.

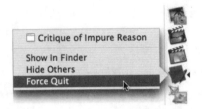

⌘-Option-Esc

Display the Force Quit Applications dialog box

Select the offending application in the Force Quit Applications dialog box and click the Force Quit button to force-quit it:

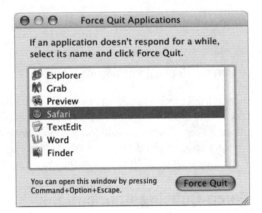

⌘-Shift-Q

Display the Log Out dialog box

Use the Log Out dialog box (shown here) to log out manually. You can also display the Log Out dialog box by choosing | Log Out. Click the Log Out button to log out immediately. If you leave the Log Out dialog box displayed for two minutes (for example, you press ⌘-Shift-Q and then leave your computer),

Mac OS X logs you out automatically. To prevent logout, dismiss the Log Out dialog box by clicking the Cancel button within two minutes of displaying it.

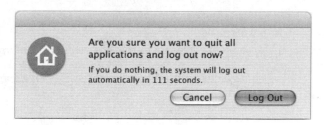

⌘-K

Display the Connect To Server dialog box

Choose the server in the Recent Servers drop-down list (click the button with the clock on it) or in the Favorite Servers list boxes, or type the server's address in the Server Address text box. Click the Connect button to connect to the server.

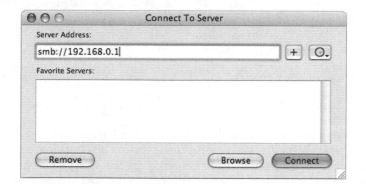

⌘-E

Eject the selected drive

This shortcut ejects the drive or other object that you've mounted as a volume on the desktop. The object can be a CD or other optical disc, a network drive, an iPod, a disk image (DMG) file, or various other types of devices.

》 Note: *Some Macs also support pressing* F12 *to eject the selected drive.*

Deleting and Trashing Items

If you exercise the creative freedom that your Mac gives you, sooner or later you'll need to delete some files and folders. You can do so directly from the keyboard by using shortcuts.

Mac OS X, Finder, and Safari

Shortcuts for Deleting and Trashing Items

⌘-Delete

Move the selected item to the Trash

Mac OS X moves the selected file or folder to the Trash without confirmation.

≫ Note: *You can undo a move to the Trash by pressing ⌘-Z or choosing Edit | Undo Move.*

⌘-Shift-Delete

Empty the Trash

Using this shortcut (or issuing an Empty Trash command from the Finder menu) makes Mac OS X display a confirmation dialog box, as shown here. Click the OK button to get rid of everything in the Trash permanently.

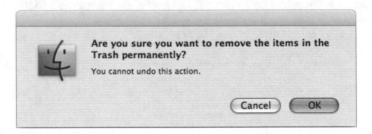

≫ Tip: *To empty the Trash without displaying this confirmation dialog box, press ⌘-Option-Shift-Delete. (In many cases, you can add Option to a key combination to suppress a confirmation dialog box that would otherwise appear.) Alternatively, right-click the Trash icon on the Dock to display the shortcut menu, and then choose the Empty Trash item.*

Working with the Dock

The Dock is designed for use with the mouse, but you can access it via the keyboard by using Mac OS X's Full Keyboard Access feature (see "Using Full Keyboard Access," later in this chapter). You can also toggle hiding on the Dock, and modify its behavior, by using keyboard shortcuts together with your mouse clicks.

Shortcuts for Working with the Dock

⌘-Option-D

Toggle hiding on the Dock

This shortcut is much quicker than choosing | Dock | Turn Hiding On (or Turn Hiding Off).

⌘-H

Hide the active application

Press this shortcut with the focus in the active application (the application you want to hide).

⌘-Option-H

Hide all other applications but the active application

This shortcut is a great way to clear your desktop so that you see only the application you're currently working in. Again, press this shortcut with the focus in the active application.

Option-click an application's Dock icon

Display the clicked application, but hide the previously active application

When you use this keyboard shortcut, Mac OS X hides all the windows of the application that was previously active.

⌘-Option-click an application's Dock icon

Display the clicked application, but hide all other running applications

When you use this keyboard shortcut, Mac OS X hides all the windows of all other running applications. This shortcut is particularly useful for applications that don't have a Hide Others command.

⌘-click a Dock icon

Open a Finder window to the folder containing that item

Control-click the Dock divider bar

Display the Dock's shortcut menu

Control-click the divider bar on the Dock to display the shortcut menu:

⌘-drag an icon to the Dock

Place the item on the Dock

Normally, when you drag an icon to the Dock, the current icons move aside to make space for the new icon. You may find that you can position the icon more easily by holding down ⌘ as you drag, which makes the current icons stay in place until after you drop the icon you're dragging.

⌘-Option-drag a document icon to a Dock icon

Force the application to open the document

Drag a document icon from the desktop or from a Finder window to an application's icon in the Dock to force that application to open the document. This technique is useful for opening a document in an application other than its default application.

Navigating the Finder

The Finder offers three main views: Icon view, List view, and Column view. Each view displays a different set of information and offers different means of keyboard navigation.

Shortcuts for Basic Navigation in the Finder

⌘-N

Open a new Finder window

> **Tip:** *To control the size at which Mac OS X opens each new Finder window, close all Finder windows, and then press ⌘-N to open a new Finder window. Drag the window to where you want it to appear, and resize it to your preferred size. Then press ⌘-W to close the window without doing anything else in it. Thereafter, Mac OS X opens new Finder windows to that size and position.*

⌘-↑

Open the parent folder of the current folder

The *parent* is the folder that contains another folder (the other folder is a *child* folder) or a file.

> **Tip:** *To display your Home folder, select the desktop and press ⌘-↑. (Your Home folder is the parent of your Desktop folder.)*

⌘-Shift-G

Display the Go To Folder dialog box

Enter the path in the Go To The Folder text box in the Go To Folder dialog box (shown here), and then click the Go button to display that folder in a Finder window. You can press Tab after typing enough letters to identify each folder in the path to make AutoComplete enter the rest of the folder's name.

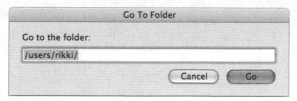

⌘-B

Toggle the display of the toolbar

This shortcut has the same effect as clicking the oval button on the toolbar or choosing either View | Show Toolbar or View | Hide Toolbar.

⌘-F

Display the Find dialog box

Shortcuts for Changing the View in the Finder

Instead of using the Icon View button, the List View button, or the Column View button on the toolbar of a Finder window, you can use these keyboard shortcuts to change views.

⌘-1

Display the active Finder window in Icon view

Icon view displays an icon for each file or folder:

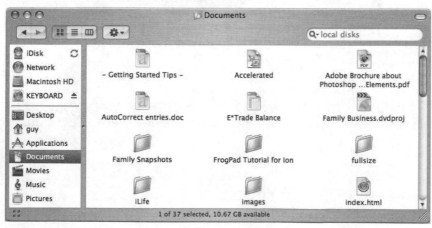

Mac OS X, Finder, and Safari

⌘-②

Display the active Finder window in List view

List view displays a vertical list of files and folders, as shown here. You can expand a folder listing by clicking the right-pointing triangle beside it, and collapse an expanded listing by clicking the resulting down-pointing triangle.

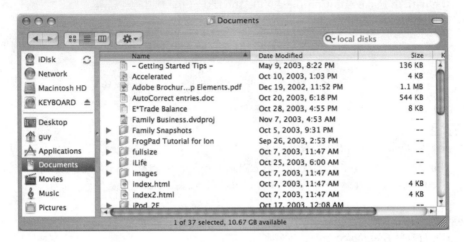

⌘-③

Display the active Finder window in Column view

Column view displays folders and files in a series of panels, as shown here:

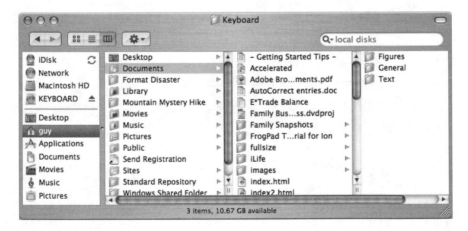

Shortcuts for Working with Aliases

 ⌘-L

Create an alias for the selected object

Mac OS X creates the alias in the same folder as the object and names it with the object's name followed by "alias". After creating the alias, drag it to the desktop or the folder in which you want it to appear.

⌘-R

Display the original for the selected alias

Select the alias and then press this shortcut to display its original in a Finder window. (Alternatively, choose File | Show Original.)

Shortcuts for Navigating in Icon View

←, →, ↑, ↓

Navigate from icon to icon

Press the appropriate arrow key to move the selection to the next icon in that direction.

 Shift-←, Shift-→, Shift-↑, Shift-↓

Select the next object in that direction

For example, if you select a file, and then press Shift-→, the Finder adds the object to that file's right to the selection.

⌘-drag

Move the icon, overriding your current Snap To Grid setting

The Snap To Grid check box in the Options dialog box for a Finder window (⌘-J or View | Show View Options) controls whether Mac OS X aligns icons according to an invisible underlying grid. ⌘-drag an icon to move it to a new position, overriding your current Snap To Grid setting.

》 Note: *You can ⌘-drag to override the Snap To Grid setting on the desktop as well as in a Finder window.*

Mac OS X, Finder, and Safari

Shortcuts for Navigating in List View

[↓]

Select the next item downward in the list

[↑]

Select the next item upward in the list

[→]

Expand a folder listing

[←]

Collapse a folder listing

[Option]-click a triangle

Open all the folders within the folder

Click the gray horizontal triangle beside a folder to display all the folders inside that folder and their contents.

≫ Tip: [⌘]-*click to select multiple folders; then* [Option]-*click a gray horizontal triangle to expand all the folders and files in all the selected folders.*

[Control]-[Tab]

Select the next column in List view

When you press this shortcut, Mac OS X selects the next column heading and sorts the list by that column.

[Control]-[Shift]-[Tab]

Select the previous column in List view

When you press this shortcut, Mac OS X selects the previous column heading and sorts the list by that column.

Shortcuts for Navigating in Column View

[↑]

Select the next item up

[↓]

Select the next item down

→

Move to the next pane to the right

←

Move to the next pane to the left

⌘-[

Go back to the previous location

⌘-]

Go forward again to the previous forward location

⌘-O, ⌘-↓

Open the current item

Option-drag a column handle

Change the width of all columns at the same time

Option-drag a column handle, as shown here, to change the width of all columns at the same time. (To change the width of only the column you drag, drag its column handle.)

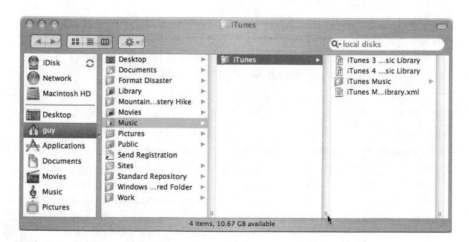

Option

Display the full name of the file the mouse pointer is over

Alternatively, hover the mouse pointer for a second or so until Mac OS X displays the pop-up containing the filename. Pressing Option is quicker.

Using Full Keyboard Access

Mac OS X includes a feature named Full Keyboard Access that lets you access the Mac OS X menu bar, Dock, and other parts of the screen using your keyboard. Depending on how your Mac is configured, you'll probably need to turn on Full Keyboard Access before you can use it.

» *Tip:* *When using the Full Keyboard Access shortcuts on a PowerBook or iBook, hold down* Control *first, and then hold down* Fn *while you press the appropriate function key.*

Shortcuts for Using Full Keyboard Access

Control - F1

Toggle Full Keyboard Access on and off

» *Note:* *You can also turn Full Keyboard Access on and off by choosing* ⬛ | *System Preferences, clicking the Keyboard & Mouse icon in the Hardware section to display the Keyboard & Mouse sheet, and selecting or clearing the Turn On Full Keyboard Access check box on the Keyboard Shortcuts tab. As usual, the keyboard shortcut is much quicker.*

Control - F2

Select the menu bar

When you press Control - F2 to select the menu bar, Mac OS X displays the ⬛ menu, the first item on the menu bar. Press → (and if necessary ←) to display the appropriate command; then press ↓ (and if necessary ↑) to select the command. Then press Return to invoke the command.

Control - F3

Select the Dock

When you press Control - F3 to select the Dock, Mac OS X selects an icon on the Dock. Press ←, →, ↑, or ↓ to select the icon you want, and then press Return to activate it. To display a shortcut menu for an icon, press the arrow key pointing toward the middle of the screen. (For example, if the Dock is positioned along the bottom of the screen, press ↑ to display the shortcut menu.) Use ←, →, ↑, or ↓ to navigate to the appropriate command, and then press Return to invoke the command.

Control - F4

Select the active window or the window behind it

The first press of Control - F4 selects the active window. The next press selects the window behind the active window.

⌜Control⌝-⌜F5⌝

Select the toolbar

When you press ⌜Control⌝-⌜F5⌝ to select the toolbar, Mac OS X displays a thin blue outline around the first button on the toolbar. Press ⌜Tab⌝ to move the outline to the next button; press ⌜Control⌝-⌜Tab⌝ to move the outline to the previous button. Press ⌜Return⌝ to click the selected button.

⌜Control⌝-⌜F6⌝

Select a tool palette

When you press ⌜Control⌝-⌜F6⌝, Mac OS X selects the first tool palette in the application. Press ⌜Control⌝-⌜F6⌝ again to select the next tool palette.

⌜Control⌝-⌜F7⌝

Select an available control in the active dialog box

Press ⌜Control⌝-⌜F7⌝ as many times as necessary to select the control you want to work with.

Using Zoom and Other Visual Enhancements

To make objects on screen easier to see, Mac OS X provides a powerful zoom feature, the capability to toggle to reverse video and back, and variable contrast. You can use these features by pressing the keyboard shortcuts listed below or by working on the Seeing tab of the Universal Access sheet in System Preferences (choose | System Preferences, click the Universal Access icon, and then click the Seeing tab button).

Shortcuts for Visual Enhancements

⌜⌘⌝-⌜Option⌝-⌜8⌝

Toggle zooming on and off

Zooming is off by default. Press this shortcut to turn it on when you need to zoom in or out.

⌜⌘⌝-⌜Option⌝-⌜]⌝

Zoom in

Press this shortcut as many times as necessary to zoom in to the degree you need.

⌜⌘⌝-⌜Option⌝-⌜[⌝

Zoom out

Press this shortcut as many times as necessary to zoom out.

Mac OS X, Finder, and Safari

⌘-Option-Control-8
Toggle White On Black and Black On White

Press this shortcut to switch from the default Black On White to White On Black (reverse video). Press this shortcut again to switch back.

⌘-Option-Control-V
Increase the contrast

》Note: *⌘-Option-Control-V and ⌘-Option-Control-W may not work on all Macs.*

⌘-Option-Control-W
Reduce the contrast

Creating a Spoken Command for a Keyboard Shortcut

If your place of work or play is quiet enough for you to use spoken commands to control your Mac (or if you're free to yell at your Mac without distressing anyone), you can create a spoken command that performs a keyboard shortcut. Using spoken commands like this can be a great way of performing keyboard shortcuts that you find awkward to press or impossible to remember.

To create a spoken command for a keyboard shortcut, first turn on Apple Speakable Items and configure your Mac for listening. To do so, follow these steps:

1. Choose | System Preferences to display the System Preferences window.
2. Click the Speech item in the System area to display the Speech sheet.
3. On the Speech Recognition tab, click the On/Off button to display its subsheet:

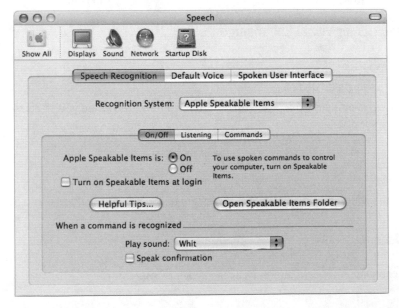

4. In the Apple Speakable Items Is area, select the On option button.

5. Click the Listening button to display its subsheet:

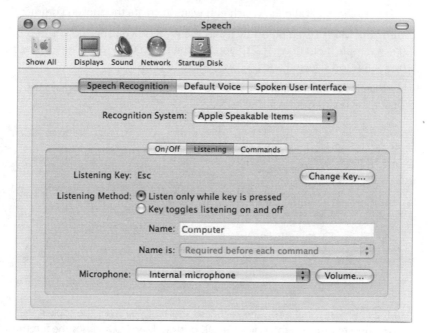

6. Use the controls on the Listening subsheet to change your Mac's listening configuration if necessary:

- In the Listening Method area, select the Listen Only While Key Is Pressed option button (the default) or the Key Toggles Listening On And Off option button to suit your preference.

- To change the key used for listening, click the Change Key button and use the resulting panel to set the key (or keys) you want to use. Then click the OK button to return to the Listening subsheet.

- If you select the Key Toggles Listening On And Off option button, change the name in the Name text box (the default name is *Computer*) as necessary. Then choose the appropriate setting in the Name Is drop-down list: Optional Before Commands, Required Before Each Command, Required 15 Seconds After Last Command, or Required 30 Seconds After Last Command. (You may need to experiment with these settings to find which works best for your listening needs and the place you're using your Mac.)

- In the Microphone drop-down list, make sure the appropriate microphone is selected. If necessary, click the Volume button and use the resulting Microphone Volume dialog box to change the microphone volume. Click the Done button when you've finished.

After turning on Apple Speakable Items and configuring Listening, you're ready to create the spoken command. Follow these steps:

1. Switch to the application in which you want to create the spoken command.

2. Turn your Mac's Listening on by using the method you specified in step 6. (For example, hold down (Esc) if you left the Listen Only While Key Is Pressed option button selected and (Esc) as the key to press.)

3. Say "Define a keyboard command" to your Mac. Mac OS X displays the Define Keyboard Command window:

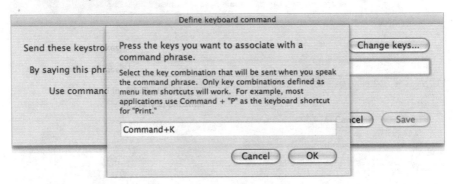

4. In the foremost panel, press the keyboard shortcut you want the spoken command to run, and then click the OK button. Mac OS X closes the foremost panel, revealing the rest of the Define Keyboard Command dialog box:

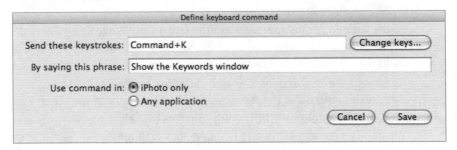

5. Type the command phrase in the By Saving This Phrase text box.

6. In the Use Command In area, select the *Application* Only option button (where *Application* is the name of the application you're working in) or the Any Application option button as appropriate.

7. Click the Save button to close the Define Keyboard Command dialog box and create the command.

Switch to the application (if necessary) and test the spoken command to make sure it works.

Logging Out, Sleeping, Restarting, and Shutting Down

Instead of using the menu, you can use keyboard shortcuts to log out, put your Mac to sleep, restart your Mac, or shut your Mac down.

Shortcuts for Logging Out, Sleeping, Restarting, and Shutting Down

⌘-Shift-Q

Log the current user out

When you press this shortcut, Mac OS X displays the confirmation dialog box shown here. Click the Log Out button or leave your Mac alone for two minutes to log out. Click the Cancel button if you displayed this dialog box by mistake.

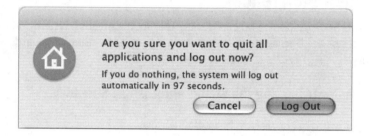

⌘-Option-Shift-Q

Log out without displaying the confirmation dialog box

Power button, Control-Eject, Control-F12

Put your Mac to sleep, restart it, or shut it down

When you press any of these shortcuts, Mac OS X displays the confirmation dialog box shown here. Press ⒮ or click the Sleep button to sleep, press ⓇR or click the Restart button to restart, or press Return or click the Shut Down button to shut down.

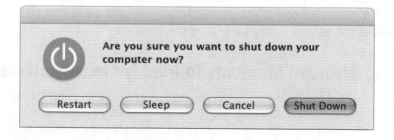

>> **Note:** *Pressing the Power button produces this effect only on an iBook or PowerBook. Pressing the Power button on a desktop Mac puts it to sleep. Hold down the Power button to power down a 'Book or a desktop Mac.*

⌘-Control-Option-Eject, ⌘-Control-Option-F12

Shut down your Mac without displaying the confirmation dialog box

Control-Option-Eject, Control-Option-F12

Restart your Mac

Displaying the Sound and Display Sheets in System Preferences

On a PowerBook or iBook, you can display the Sound sheet in System Preferences or the Display sheet in System Preferences by using keyboard shortcuts.

Shortcuts for Displaying the Sound and Display Sheets

Option-F3, Option-F4, Option-F5

Display the Sound sheet in System Preferences

On a standard PowerBook or iBook keyboard, F3 is the Mute key, F4 is the Decrease Volume key, and F5 is the Increase Volume key. Press Option and any one of these keys without pressing Fn to display the Sound sheet.

>> **Tip:** *On a desktop Mac, press Option and one of the volume keys to display the Sound sheet.*

Option-F1, Option-F2

Display the Display sheet in System Preferences

On a standard PowerBook or iBook keyboard, F1 is the Decrease Brightness key and F2 is the Increase Brightness key. Press Option and either of these keys without pressing Fn to display the Display sheet.

Using Keyboard Shortcuts to Modify Mouse Actions

As mentioned at the beginning of this chapter, you can use the modifier keys to modify mouse actions in Mac OS X. These aren't exactly keyboard shortcuts because they involve the mouse, but because they use the keyboard to deliver additional functionality, they qualify as honorary keyboard shortcuts here. (In any case, you'll find them useful.)

Shortcuts for Modifying Mouse Actions

[Option]-click in the scroll bar
Override the Click In The Scroll Bar To setting

[Option]-click in the scroll bar to override your setting in the Click In The Scroll Bar To area of the Appearance sheet of System Preferences. (To display the Appearance sheet, choose | System Preferences, and then click the Appearance icon.) Mac OS X offers you the choice between having a click in the scroll bar display the next page (select the Jump To The Next Page option button) or scroll to the point in the document corresponding to the point where you click in the scroll bar (select the Scroll To Here option button).

» Note: *[Option]-clicking in the scroll bar and [Option]-dragging the thumb work only in Cocoa (Mac OS X-native) applications.*

[Option]-drag the thumb
Scroll more slowly than usual

Hold down [Option] while you drag the *thumb* (the handle in the scroll bar) to scroll more slowly.

[Option]-click the scroll arrows
Scroll by pages rather than by lines

[⌘]-[Option]-drag
Scroll the window in the direction you drag

Instead of scrolling horizontally and then vertically to reach the part of the window you need, you can scroll diagonally by [⌘]-[Option]-dragging.

[Option]-drag a menulet
Move or remove a menulet

The *menulets* are the menus at the right end of the menu bar. [Option]-drag a menulet to the left or right to reposition it. [Option]-drag a menulet off the menu bar to remove it.

[⌘]-click a folder on the toolbar
Open the folder in a new window

Use this shortcut when you want to keep the current folder open in its own window and open the other folder in a new window.

Mac OS X, Finder, and Safari

Option -click a folder on the toolbar

Open the folder in a new window, but close the current window

Use this shortcut when you want to close the window for the current folder and open the other folder in a new window of its own.

Option -drag an item

Copy the item instead of moving it

Spacebar

Open a spring-loaded folder when you've turned off spring-loaded folders

When you clear the Spring-Loaded Folders And Windows check box on the General tab of the Preferences dialog box (⌘-,) for the Finder, you can press Spacebar to trigger the spring-loaded action.

Capturing the Screen

You can use the following keyboard shortcuts to capture all or part of the screen. These shortcuts create a PDF file named Picture *n*, where *n* is the next available unused number, on your desktop: Picture 1, Picture 2, and so on.

Shortcuts for Capturing the Screen

⌘ - Shift - 3

Capture your entire screen

⌘ - Shift - 4

Capture a rectangle of your choice

When you press this shortcut, Mac OS X changes the mouse pointer to a crosshair. Click and drag to select the rectangle you want to capture, and then release the mouse button to take the snap.

⌘ - Shift - 4 , then Spacebar

Capture the specified window or the Dock

When you press ⌘-Shift-4, Mac OS X changes the mouse pointer to a crosshair. Press Spacebar to make Mac OS X change the crosshair to a camera. Click the window you want to capture. Click between icons on the Dock to capture the Dock.

Internet Explorer Shortcuts

You can use shortcuts to control Internet Explorer from the keyboard.

Shortcuts for Internet Explorer

⌘-R

Refresh the current page

Pressing this shortcut has the same effect as clicking the Refresh button on the Button bar.

⌘-T

Toggle the display of the Explorer bar

⌘-B

Collapse or expand toolbars

Press this highly useful shortcut to toggle the toolbars between collapsed (which gives you more space to view pages) and expanded (which gives you access to the toolbar buttons).

⌘-;

Display the Internet Explorer Preferences dialog box

Unlike most applications, Internet Explorer doesn't use the ⌘-, keyboard shortcut to display its Preferences dialog box. (Instead, ⌘-, displays the Auction Manager window.)

↑

Scroll up

↓

Scroll down

Spacebar

Scroll down one page

Option-Spacebar

Scroll up one page

Mac OS X, Finder, and Safari

⌘-drag in an empty area of the page
Scroll the page in the direction you drag

⌘-click a link
Open the link in a new window

This method of opening a link in a new window tends to be more convenient than right-clicking the link and choosing Open Link In New Window from the shortcut menu.

⌘-Return
Open the URL in a new window

Type the URL in the Address bar as usual, and then press ⌘-Return to open it in a new window instead of pressing Return to open it in the current window.

Option-click a link
Download the link to disk

Internet Explorer saves the file in the file specified in the Download Folder group box on the Download Options page of the Internet Explorer Preferences dialog box. (The default location is your Desktop folder.)

Safari Keyboard Shortcuts

Safari provides a wealth of keyboard shortcuts for controlling most aspects of browsing.

Shortcuts for Navigating in Safari

You can use the following shortcuts to navigate in Safari when the focus is on the page background.

⌘-Home, ⌘-Shift-H
Display your Home page

To set your Home page, press ⌘-,, or choose Safari | Preferences to display the Preferences dialog box, and then enter the URL in the Home Page text box on the General sheet.

⌘-.
Stop loading the active page

⸤Spacebar⸥

Scroll down by a screenful

When you press ⸤Spacebar⸥ to scroll down, Safari leaves a small overlap so that you can see part of the screen that was previously displayed.

⸤←⸥, ⸤→⸥, ⸤↑⸥, ⸤↓⸥

Scroll upward, downward, left, or right by a small amount

⸤Option⸥-⸤←⸥, ⸤Option⸥-⸤→⸥, ⸤Option⸥-⸤↑⸥, ⸤Option⸥-⸤↓⸥

Scroll left, right, up, or down by a screenful

When you press one of these keyboard shortcuts, Safari scrolls by a little less than a screenful so that you can still see part of the screen that was previously displayed.

⸤Page Up⸥

Scroll upward by a screenful

⸤Page Down⸥

Scroll downward by a screenful

⸤⌘⸥-⸤↑⸥, ⸤Home⸥

Scroll to the upper-left corner of the page

⸤⌘⸥-⸤↓⸥, ⸤End⸥

Scroll to the lower-left corner of the page

⸤Delete⸥

Go back to the previous page

⸤Shift⸥-⸤Delete⸥

Go forward to the next page

⸤⌘⸥-click a link

Open the link in a new window

Mac OS X, Finder, and Safari

⌘-Shift-click a link

Open the link in a new window behind the active window

This shortcut is useful when you want to follow one or more links from the active window but finish reading the contents of the active window before reading the linked contents.

⌘-Return

Open the URL in a new window

Type the URL in the Address bar as usual, and then press ⌘-Return to open it in a new window instead of pressing Return to open it in the current window.

⌘-Shift-Return in the Address field

Open the URL in a new window behind the active window

⌘-Return in the Search field

Search and return the results in a new window

⌘-Shift-Return in the Search field

Search and return the results in a new window behind the active window

Option-click and hold Back button

Display the last ten pages visited, listed by URL

Clicking and holding the Back button displays the pages listed by page title. Option-click and hold to display them listed by URL instead.

Option-click and hold Forward button

Display the next ten pages forward, listed by URL

Clicking and holding the Forward button displays the pages listed by page title. Option-click and hold to display them listed by URL instead.

⌘-A

Select all of the current page

Shortcuts for Configuring Safari

You can use the following keyboard shortcuts to configure Safari and control which parts of its interface are displayed.

⌘-[]

Toggle the display of the Address bar

⌘-B

Toggle the display of the Favorites bar

⌘-/

Toggle the display of the status bar

⌘-K

Toggle blocking of pop-up windows

Switch on blocking by pressing this shortcut or by choosing Safari | Block Pop-Up Windows to prevent pop-up windows (such as ads) from appearing.

⌘-+

Make the text bigger

⌘-−

Make the text smaller

⌘-Shift-P

Display the Page Setup sheet

⌘-Option-E

Empty the Safari cache

When you press this shortcut (or choose File | Empty Cache), Safari displays the confirmation dialog box shown here to make sure you know what you're doing. Click the Empty button if you want to proceed.

Are you sure you want to empty the cache?

Safari saves the contents of web pages you open in a cache so that it's faster to visit them again.

Cancel   Empty

⌘-Shift-V

View the source code for the active page

Mac OS X, Finder, and Safari

≫ Tip: *To set the default size and position for Safari windows, quit Safari (⌘-Q)*
and restart it so that it has just one window open. Change that window to the
right size, and move it to the right position. Then quit Safari again. When you
restart Safari, it will use that size and position for new windows.

Shortcuts for Finding and Searching in Safari

⌘-E

Find the selected text

⌘-F

Display the Find dialog box

Enter the search term in the Find dialog box and click the Previous button or the
Next button as appropriate.

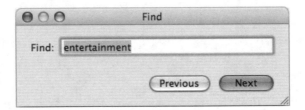

⌘-G

Find the next instance of the search term

Press this shortcut to find the next instance of the current search term without
displaying the Find dialog box.

⌘-Shift-G

Find the previous instance of the search term

Press this shortcut to find the previous instance of the current search term
without displaying the Find dialog box.

⌘-Option-F

Select the Google Search box

⌘-N

Open a new Safari window to your Home page

⌘-Ⓛ

Select the address in the Address bar

Press this shortcut to select the current contents of the Address bar so that you can type over them or edit them.

⌘-Ⓡ

Refresh the active page

This shortcut has the same effect as clicking the Reload button on the toolbar or choosing View | Reload Page.

⌘-Ⓢ

Display the Save As sheet

⌘-Shift-Ⓝ

Display the Bookmarks bar and create a new bookmark folder

Safari assigns the new folder the provisional name *untitled folder* and displays an edit box around the name so that you can change it immediately. Type the new name and press Return to enter it.

Shortcuts for Displaying and Hiding Windows

⌘-Option-Ⓐ

Display the Activity window

The Activity window (shown here) enables you to see which pages you've accessed or are accessing. This shortcut displays the Activity window but doesn't hide it again; to get rid of the Activity window, click its close button (the red button).

Activity	
Address	**Status**
▶ Mac Rumors: Apple Mac Rumors and News You Care About	29 items
▼ iTunes Music Store Downloads Top 25 Million Songs	27 items
http://a772.g.akamai.net/7/772/5....apple.com/t/2002/us/en/i/7.gif	1.8 KB
http://a772.g.akamai.net/7/772/5....apple.com/t/2002/us/en/i/4.gif	1.6 KB
http://a772.g.akamai.net/7/772/5...e.com/t/2002/us/en/i/1.1left.gif	0.4 KB
http://a772.g.akamai.net/7/772/5...n/elements/singlepixela1a5a9.gif	43 bytes
http://a772.g.akamai.net/7/772/5...ple.com/t/2002/us/en/i/1.1b.gif	0.7 KB
http://a772.g.akamai.net/7/772/5....apple.com/t/2002/us/en/i/2.gif	1.6 KB
http://a772.g.akamai.net/7/772/5....com/t/2002/us/en/i/1bg.gif (4)	0.4 KB
http://a772.g.akamai.net/7/772/5...com/t/2002/us/en/i/1.1right.gif	0.3 KB

Mac OS X, Finder, and Safari

⌘-Option-L

Display the Downloads window

Use the Downloads window to track the progress of your downloads. This shortcut displays the Downloads window but doesn't hide it again; to get rid of the Downloads window, click its close button (the red button).

Shortcuts for Working with Bookmarks in Safari

⌘-D

Display the Add Bookmark pane

⌘-Shift-D

Create a bookmark for the active page on the Bookmarks menu

Shift-click the Add Bookmark button

Add the bookmark directly to the Bookmarks menu

⌘-Option-B

Toggle the display of the Bookmarks window

The Bookmarks window is the most effective way of organizing your bookmarks and navigating through them.

⌘-1 to 9

Go to the bookmark with the corresponding number

Press ⌘-1 to go to the first bookmark (from the left) on your Bookmarks bar, ⌘-2 to go to the second bookmark, and so on.

⌘-click a Bookmarks folder

Open all bookmarks contained in that folder

Safari opens the bookmarks as tabs in the active window.

⌘-double-click

Open the selected bookmark in a new window

Option-click the New Folder button

Put the selected bookmarks in a new folder

Select the bookmarks you want to affect before Option-clicking the New Folder button.

Shortcuts for Using History and SnapBack

Like most browsers, Safari provides a powerful History feature that enables you to find pages you've visited recently. Safari also includes a SnapBack feature that lets you quickly return to the page that you first displayed in a particular window (or to a page that you manually mark for SnapBack) and to your latest search results in a window.

⌘-[

Go back to the previous page

⌘-]

Go forward to the next page

⌘-Shift-H

Go to your Home page

To set your Home page, press ⌘-[, or choose Safari | Preferences to display the Preferences dialog box, and then enter the URL in the Home Page text box on the General sheet.

⌘-Option-M

Mark the active page for SnapBack

When you open a new Safari window, Safari automatically marks the first page you load in that window as the SnapBack page for that window. You can snap back to that page by clicking the white arrow in the orange circle at the right end of the Address bar. This shortcut marks the active page for SnapBack in the

Mac OS X, Finder, and Safari

active window instead of the previous SnapBack page for that window. Alternatively, you can choose History | Mark Page For SnapBack.

⌘-Option-P

Return to the SnapBack page for the active window

Pressing this shortcut is the equivalent of clicking the SnapBack arrow in the Address bar or choosing History | Page SnapBack.

⌘-Option-S

Return to the SnapBack page for search results

Pressing this shortcut is the equivalent of clicking the SnapBack arrow in the Search box or choosing History | Search Results SnapBack.

Shortcuts for Using Tabs in Safari

If you use Safari's Tabs feature, you can use the following keyboard shortcuts to work with tabs and navigate among them. To turn tabs on, press ⌘-, to display the Preferences dialog box, click the Tabs button to display its sheet, and select the Enable Tabbed Browsing check box.

⌘-click a link

Open the linked page in a new tab

⌘-Shift-click a link

Open the linked page in a new tab and select it

⌘-Shift-←

Select the previous tab

⌘-Shift-→

Select the next tab

3

Office's Shared Keyboard Shortcuts and AutoCorrect

This chapter explains the keyboard shortcuts that are shared among all or most of the Office v.X applications. Discussing these shortcuts together for all the applications lets you learn the most common shortcuts more easily, without needing to dig through the separate chapter for each application. This chapter also discusses the keystroke-saving tool that all the Office applications share: AutoCorrect. Word's implementation of AutoCorrect has more features than the other applications' implementations, but the basis of AutoCorrect is the same in each application, so we can save pages and effort by discussing it here rather than in the following chapters.

The following chapters, which discuss the individual applications and the shortcuts they offer, mention the shared keyboard shortcuts again briefly when a shared shortcut needs further explanation or behaves differently in an application.

Shared Keyboard Shortcuts

The Office v.X applications—Word, Excel, PowerPoint, and Entourage—share many keyboard shortcuts for common tasks such as opening and saving files, applying alignment, and undoing and redoing actions. This section presents these keyboard shortcuts by category. Not every keyboard shortcut is implemented in each application, and where a keyboard shortcut is implemented, the implementation sometimes varies according to the capabilities and needs of the application in question.

You'll notice that there are many similarities between the shared keyboard shortcuts and the standard (or more-or-less standard) Mac shortcuts discussed in the previous chapter. You'll also notice that the Office applications have some different keyboard shortcuts.

Opening, Saving, and Printing Files

Some of the first keyboard shortcuts you should learn are those for opening and saving files, actions you'll typically perform multiple times in the course of a day. You'll probably also need to print files fairly often.

Shortcuts for Opening, Saving, and Printing Files

⌘-O

Display the Open dialog box

Use this shortcut to display the Open dialog box so that you can open a file.

⌘-S

Save the active file

When you press this shortcut for a file that has never been saved before, the application displays the Save As sheet so that you can specify the filename and the folder in which to save it. After the file has a filename, pressing this shortcut saves the file under its current name in its current location.

F12

Display the Save As sheet

Use the Save As sheet to save the active file under a different name, in a different folder, or both.

⌘-P

Display the Print dialog box

In most applications, the Print dialog box offers a range of settings for printing, but you can print immediately using your current settings by pressing Return to "click" the Print button. The illustration shows the Print dialog box from Word v.X. Most applications also let you print without seeing the Print dialog box by clicking the Print button on the Standard toolbar.

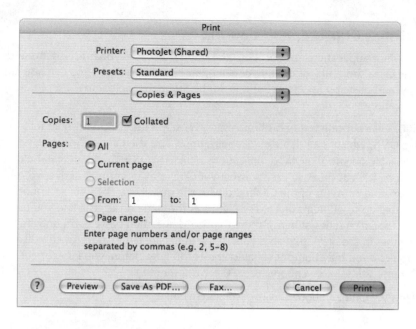

Applying Alignment

You can apply alignment from the keyboard in all the Office applications instead of using the corresponding buttons on the Formatting toolbar.

Shortcuts for Applying Alignment

⌘-Ⓛ

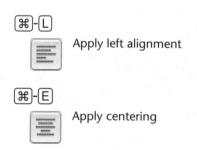

Apply left alignment

⌘-Ⓔ

Apply centering

⌘-Ⓡ

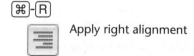

Apply right alignment

Cutting, Copying, and Pasting

The Office applications support both the standard Mac keyboard shortcuts and some extra shortcuts for cutting, copying, and pasting objects. You can also cut, copy, and paste by using the buttons on the Standard toolbar in most of the applications.

Office uses not one but two Clipboards—the standard Clipboard built into Mac OS X, which is available to all applications, and the Office Clipboard, which is available only to the Office applications. The Mac OS X Clipboard can hold only one item at once, so each subsequent Copy or Cut command overwrites the existing contents of the Clipboard with the new item. The Office Clipboard can hold up to 60 items or 16MB of items at the same time, enabling you to copy (or cut) a series of items to the Clipboard and then paste them one after the other in the order that suits you. (If the items are large—such as complex graphics—you may bump up against the 16MB limit before you copy or cut 60 items. But for conventional use, 60 items is plenty.)

Here's the Office Clipboard with several items on it:

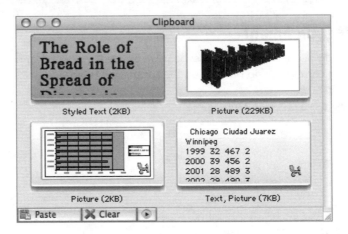

Here's how to use the Office Clipboard:

- Choose View | Office Clipboard to display the Office Clipboard so that you can start copying or cutting items to it. (Copying or cutting an item without the Office Clipboard displayed places the item only on the Mac OS X Clipboard.)
- Select an item and copy it (for example, press ⌘-Ⓒ) or cut it (for example, press ⌘-Ⓧ) as usual.
- To see what's on the Office Clipboard, scroll up and down to see items that don't fit within the display, drag the sizing handle to resize it to multiple columns, or do both.

- To paste an item, activate the appropriate application and position the insertion point where you want the item to appear, select the item on the Office Clipboard, and then issue a Paste command (for example, press ⌘-Ⓥ) or click the Paste button.

- To paste all items, position the insertion point and choose Paste All from the drop-down menu:

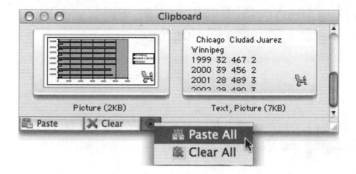

- To clear the Office Clipboard of all its current contents, choose Clear All from the drop-down menu.

- To delete an item, Control-click or right-click it and choose Clear from the shortcut menu.

When you paste an item, Office retains as much of the formatting as possible. If you don't get the result you want, undo the Paste operation (press ⌘-Ⓩ), choose Edit | Paste Special to display the Paste Special dialog box, and select a different paste format from those available.

Shortcuts for Cutting, Copying, and Pasting

Control-Ⓒ, F3

Copy the current selection to the Mac OS X Clipboard and the Office Clipboard (if displayed)

Control-Ⓥ, F4

Paste the current contents of the Mac OS X Clipboard or the selected item from the Office Clipboard

 To paste an item from the Office Clipboard, select it, and then press this shortcut.

Shared Shortcuts and AutoCorrect

Control-X, F2

Cut the current selection to the Mac OS X Clipboard and the Office Clipboard (if displayed)

Launching the Visual Basic Editor and Displaying the Macros Dialog box

Word, Excel, and PowerPoint support Visual Basic for Applications (VBA), the programming language built into Office for recording macros and writing code. Entourage doesn't currently support VBA.

Shortcuts for Launching the Visual Basic Editor and Displaying the Macros Dialog Box

Option-F11

Display the Visual Basic Editor

Option-F8

Display the Macros dialog box

From the Macros dialog box, you can run an existing macro or open a macro for editing in the Visual Basic Editor. The advantage to opening the Visual Basic Editor via the Macros dialog box rather than directly via the Option-F11 keyboard shortcut is that you can make Visual Basic display the macro you want to edit, rather than having to navigate to it manually.

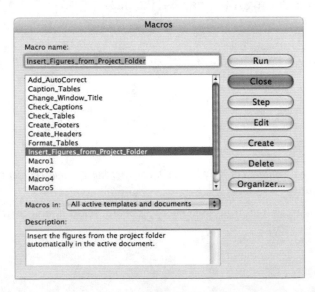

Undoing, Redoing, and Repeating Actions

The Office applications support standard Mac OS X keyboard shortcuts for undoing actions, redoing undone actions, and repeating the last action.

Shortcuts for Undoing, Redoing, and Repeating Actions

⌘-Z

Undo the previous action

Most of the Office applications support multiple levels of Undo. Each ⌘-Z keypress undoes one action, so you can undo multiple actions by issuing the shortcut multiple times.

⌘-Y

Redo or repeat the previous action

If you've just undone an action, this shortcut redoes the action. If not, this shortcut repeats the previous action. If you're not sure which action will be redone or repeated when you issue this shortcut, display the Edit menu and check the second command, which will read "Redo Delete," "Redo Typing '4' in A7," or a similar brief description.

Invoking Frequently Used Tools

The Office applications provide keyboard shortcuts for displaying the Find dialog box (or the Find tab of the Find And Replace dialog box), displaying the Insert Hyperlink dialog box, and running the Spelling Checker.

Shortcuts for Invoking Frequently Used Tools

⌘-F

Display the Find dialog box or the Find tab of the Find And Replace dialog box

⌘-K

Display the Insert Hyperlink dialog box

The Insert Hyperlink dialog box (Figure 3-1) lets you insert a hyperlink at the current selection. The options available vary depending on the application. The figure shows the Insert Hyperlink dialog box for Word v.X.

F7

Run the Spelling Checker

The Spelling Checker scans the file or the current selection for spelling errors and displays suggestions for apparent errors that it finds.

Shared Shortcuts and AutoCorrect

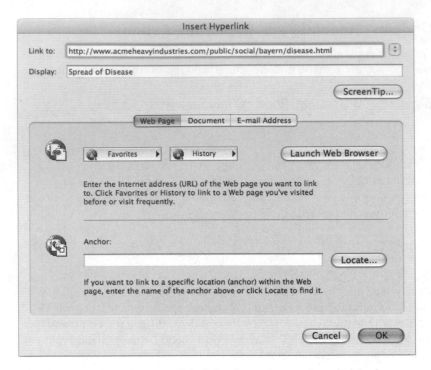

Figure 3-1   Use the Insert Hyperlink dialog box to insert a hyperlink in the active document.

» Note: Entourage uses the keyboard shortcut ⌘-Option-L to run the Spelling Checker.

Saving Keystrokes and Time with AutoCorrect

Office has the mother of all keyboard shortcuts built into it in the form of AutoCorrect. Most Office users fail to appreciate the extent of AutoCorrect's capabilities and so don't use it fully; but you, in your quest to become a keyboard-shortcut fiend, can be the exception. This section explains what AutoCorrect is, how it works, and how you can get the most out of it.

What AutoCorrect Is

If you've used the Office applications at all, you've probably bumped into AutoCorrect. It's the feature that watches as you type and makes corrections automatically when you type characters that match one of its entries. For example, if you type "abbout" and a space (or another character that triggers an AutoCorrect check), AutoCorrect automatically corrects the word to "about." Office ships with several hundred AutoCorrect entries, and you can create as many of your own entries as you want.

If you've worked with older word processing applications, you may remember what were confusingly called "glossaries." A *glossary* was a block of text that you could define an abbreviation for, type the abbreviation, and then invoke the Glossary command to substitute the text block for the abbreviation. AutoCorrect is an automatic form of glossary that runs all the time and checks each group of characters you type. Word also includes manual glossaries, which are now called AutoText.

AutoCorrect is implemented in all the Office v.X applications, but works in somewhat different ways depending on the application. Word has the most extensive implementation, including both formatted AutoCorrect entries and unformatted (text) AutoCorrect entries. The other applications use only unformatted AutoCorrect entries.

So that each application can access them, Office stores unformatted AutoCorrect entries centrally in the MS Office ACL [*Language*] file in your ~/Library/Preferences/ Microsoft folder (where *Language* is the language you're using—for example, English).

>> *Tip:* *If you use AutoCorrect extensively, and invest time and effort in creating custom AutoCorrect entries that suit your needs, back up your MS Office ACL file so that you can restore it if you have to reinstall Mac OS X. If you use multiple Macs, copy your ACL file from one computer to another so you don't need to re-create your AutoCorrect entries manually.*

Configuring AutoCorrect

To configure AutoCorrect and create and delete entries, you work in the AutoCorrect dialog box (Tools | AutoCorrect). The number of tabs in the AutoCorrect dialog box depends on the application: four tabs in Word (Figure 3-2); two tabs in Entourage, and one tab in PowerPoint and Excel.

For each application, AutoCorrect offers self-explanatory options for correcting two initial capitals, capitalizing the first letter of each sentence, and capitalizing the names of days. Setting these options is a matter of personal preference. Many people turn off the Capitalize First Letter Of Sentences option because they find it annoying when they're typing notes or composing fragments of sentences.

AutoCorrect's most important option is Replace Text As You Type, which controls whether AutoCorrect scans for entries as you type and replaces any it finds with the designated replacement text. You'll seldom want to turn this option off, unless you're using someone else's account on a Mac, and you find AutoCorrect unexpectedly replacing text you type.

How AutoCorrect Works

AutoCorrect examines each character as you type. When you type a character that typically means you've finished typing a word, AutoCorrect compares the

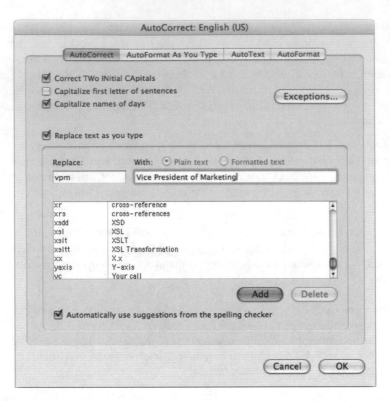

Figure 3-2 AutoCorrect can save you many keystrokes and much effort if you use it extensively.

last group of characters against its list of entries. If the group of characters matches an entry, AutoCorrect substitutes the replacement text for the word. If the group of characters doesn't match an entry, AutoCorrect checks that group of characters and the previous group of characters together to see if they match an entry. If so, AutoCorrect substitutes the replacement text. If not, AutoCorrect checks those two groups with the group before them—and so on until it has checked all the complete groups in the preceding 31 characters, at which point it gives up.

AutoCorrect entries can be up to 199 characters long and can contain spaces and punctuation. The replacement text for an entry can be up to 255 characters long—plenty to enable you to enter a short paragraph or two. (If you try to use more than 255 characters, AutoCorrect warns you that it will need to shorten the replacement text.)

No AutoCorrect entry's name should be a real word in any language you use, because otherwise AutoCorrect will replace that word each time you try to use it. The exception is if you want to *prevent* yourself from using a particular word. For example, if the word "purchase" sends your boss into a rage, you can define AutoCorrect entries to change words based on "purchase" (purchase, purchases, purchased, purchasing, and so on) to their counterparts based on "buy." AutoCorrect will then censor your writing automatically.

AutoCorrect considers various characters to mean you've finished typing a word. These characters include spaces, punctuation, tabs, carriage returns, and line feeds (Shift-Enter). Various symbols (such as % and #) also trigger AutoCorrect checks.

Creating and Deleting AutoCorrect Entries

AutoCorrect comes with a large number of built-in entries that range from simple typos (for example, "abotu" instead of "about") to basic grammatical mistakes (for example, "may of been" instead of "may have been") and some symbols (for example, AutoCorrect corrects (r) to a registered symbol, ®). You can add as many custom entries as you need. You can also replace or delete the built-in entries if you find them inconvenient.

To work with AutoCorrect entries, choose Tools | AutoCorrect to display the AutoCorrect dialog box.

Creating an AutoCorrect Entry

To create an AutoCorrect entry, follow these steps:

1. If the active document contains the replacement text for the AutoCorrect entry, select it. (Alternatively, copy the text from another application.)

2. Choose Tools | AutoCorrect to display the AutoCorrect dialog box.

3. Type the entry name in the Replace text box.

4. Type or paste the replacement text in the With text box. If you selected text in the active document in step 1, the application enters it in the With text box for you.

5. Click the Add button.

>> **Note:** *If an AutoCorrect entry with this name already exists, AutoCorrect changes the Add button to a Replace button. When you click this button, AutoCorrect prompts you to decide whether to overwrite the existing entry with the new entry.*

Deleting an AutoCorrect Entry

To delete an AutoCorrect entry, select it in the list box (scroll or type down to it) and click the Delete button.

Renaming an AutoCorrect Entry

To change the name of an existing AutoCorrect entry, select it in the list so that the application enters the entry's name in the Replace text box and its contents in the With text box. Type the new name and click the Add button to create a new entry with that name and contents. Then delete the old entry.

Shared Shortcuts and AutoCorrect

Creating AutoCorrect Entries from Misspelled Words in Word

In Word, you can also create AutoCorrect entries from misspelled words the Spelling Checker has identified:

- Control-click or right-click a word the Spelling Checker has flagged with its red underline, and then choose the correct word from the AutoCorrect submenu.
- From the Spelling And Grammar dialog box, select the correct word in the Suggestions list box, and then click the AutoCorrect button.

Word corrects the term in the text and adds an AutoCorrect entry for the misspelling.

Creating Formatted AutoCorrect Entries in Word

In Word, you can also create formatted AutoCorrect entries. These can be text entries that contain formatting, entries that consist of graphics, or both. For example, you could create a formatted AutoCorrect entry that included your company name, address, and logo.

>> Note: *Word stores formatted AutoCorrect entries in your Normal template. Avoid creating large numbers of graphical AutoCorrect entries, because doing so can bloat the Normal template and make it slow to load.*

To create a formatted AutoCorrect entry:

1. Enter the text and any graphics in a document, and apply formatting as needed.
2. Select the formatted items and choose Tools | AutoCorrect to display the AutoCorrect dialog box.
3. Make sure the Formatted Text option button in the Replace Text As You Type section of the AutoCorrect tab is selected. For a graphic, Word selects this option automatically. For formatted text that doesn't include a paragraph mark, you sometimes need to select it yourself.
4. Type the name for the entry. Don't duplicate the name for an unformatted entry—that's a recipe for confusion.
5. Click the Add button.

Undoing an AutoCorrect Correction

When AutoCorrect makes a correction that you don't want to keep, you can undo it by issuing an Undo command. (For example, press ⌘-Z or click the Undo button.)

But if you were typing fast at the time AutoCorrect made the change, you might need to undo a lot of typing (or other editing) before you can undo the AutoCorrect action. When this happens, it's easier and more efficient to undo the AutoCorrect correction manually by typing over the text.

Using AutoCorrect Effectively to Save Yourself Keystrokes

Here are three suggestions for making the most of AutoCorrect:

- **Define longer AutoCorrect entries**   AutoCorrect is wonderful for fixing typos as you type. But if you work extensively with text, consider using AutoCorrect to accelerate your typing by defining AutoCorrect entries for long words, phrases, sentences, or even paragraphs you use frequently. As mentioned earlier, the limit for an AutoCorrect entry is 255 characters, but you can use several entries in sequence. (In Word, you can also use AutoText entries instead. See Chapter 4.)

- **Use AutoCorrect for enforcing consistency**   Because AutoCorrect can change up to the preceding 199 characters, you can create AutoCorrect entries to correct whole phrases that you (or other people) get wrong. For example, if your company changes the name of its Quality Control Department to Quality Assurance Department, you might create an AutoCorrect entry to change "Quality Control Department" to "Quality Assurance Department" to help ensure the change was made throughout all documents you subsequently created. (You should probably also create a shorter AutoCorrect entry for the department's name.)

- **Create multiple AutoCorrect entries to fix the same problem**   If you create many AutoCorrect entries, remembering entries you use less frequently may be a problem. But there's nothing to stop you from creating multiple entries for the same replacement text. You can also create multiple AutoCorrect entries to fix assorted misspellings of common words. For example, you might create AutoCorrect entries to change typos such as "thoug," "thogh," "thouh," and other variations to "though."

Adding and Deleting AutoCorrect Exceptions

Once you get the hang of AutoCorrect, you'll find it an invaluable weapon in your battle against wasted keystrokes and the clock. But sometimes you'll find that AutoCorrect corrects a term you don't want it to correct. When this happens, you can prevent AutoCorrect from repeating the mistake by defining an AutoCorrect exception. To do so, click the Exceptions button on the AutoCorrect tab of the

AutoCorrect dialog box and use the controls in the AutoCorrect Exceptions dialog box (shown here).

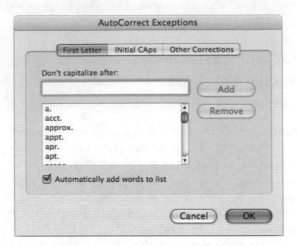

All the Office applications provide first-letter exceptions (for abbreviations such as Corp. and similar terms that end with punctuation) and initial-caps exceptions (for example, IDs). Word also provides "other exceptions," which let you define exceptions that fall outside those categories.

4

Word Keyboard Shortcuts

Of all the Office applications, Word is perhaps the best suited to using keyboard shortcuts. First, a typical Word document has more text and fewer graphical objects than a typical document in any other Office application (with the possible exception of an e-mail message in Entourage), so it's convenient to work with the keyboard. Second, Word comes with many built-in keyboard shortcuts that cover a wide variety of actions. Third, Microsoft has made Word (and Excel) very easy to customize, so you can create new keyboard shortcuts and change the built-in keyboard shortcuts as needed.

We'll start with Word's built-in shortcuts, and then move on to customizing keyboard shortcuts.

Word's Built-in Shortcuts

Word has more shortcuts than most of the other Office applications put together. This section presents them broken up into subsections by topic. We'll start with the differences worth noting about Word's implementation of the shared Office keyboard shortcuts.

Notes on the Shared Office Keyboard Shortcuts

Word uses the standard Office keyboard shortcuts discussed in "Shared Keyboard Shortcuts" in Chapter 3. The following keyboard shortcuts have differences worth noting.

Shortcuts for Creating, Opening, and Saving Documents

Word's keyboard shortcuts for creating, opening, and saving documents are standard except for the ⌘-N keyboard shortcut.

⌘-N

Create a new document using the default template

The default template is named Normal (and usually referred to as "the Normal template") and is loaded automatically when you launch Word. The Normal template contains the default settings for Word documents; for example, if you change the default font by clicking the Default button in the Font dialog box, it's the Normal template that's affected. The Normal template is stored by default in the Applications/Microsoft Office X/Templates folder on your startup disk.

Changing the View

Word offers tools for changing the view from the keyboard or using the mouse.

Shortcuts for Changing the View

⌘-Option-N

Apply Normal view

Normal view tends to be the best view for composing and editing text without worrying about its layout. You can also apply Normal view by choosing View | Normal or clicking the Normal View button on the horizontal scroll bar.

⌘-Option-O

Apply Outline view

Pressing this keyboard shortcut displays the active document in Outline view with the level of headings shown that you were last using in Outline view in this Word session. If this is the first time you've used Outline view in this Word session, you will probably need to specify the level of headings you want Word to display. (Use the keyboard shortcuts discussed next.)

You can also apply Outline view by choosing View | Outline or clicking the Outline button on the horizontal scroll bar.

Control-Shift-1 to 9

Display Outline Level 1–9

Press Control-Shift and the appropriate number for the number of heading levels you want to display. For example, press Control-Shift-1 to display Outline Level 1 paragraphs only, Control-Shift-2 to display up to Outline Level 2 paragraphs, and Control-Shift-9 to display up to Outline Level 9 paragraphs.

⌘-Option-P

Apply Page Layout view

Page Layout view displays the active document approximately as it will print with the current printer. Page Layout view is similar to Print Preview but provides fuller editing capabilities. In Page Layout view, you can see where the headers and footers will appear, where the margins will fall, and where each line will break.

You can also apply Page Layout view by choosing View | Page Layout or clicking the Print Layout View button on the horizontal scroll bar.

⌘-F2, ⌘-Option-I

Toggle Print Preview

 Print Preview displays the active document as it will print with the current printer. Print Preview provides tools for working with the margins and the page setup of the document. You can also switch to Print Preview by clicking the Print Preview button on the Standard toolbar.

While Print Preview is primarily designed for making sure your documents look right before you print hard copies of them (or fax them from your Mac), you can also use Print Preview for editing your documents. This capability is especially useful if your monitor is large enough to display two pages at once side by side, because you can see how the changes you make on the current page affect the next page.

 By default, Word switches to Magnifier mode when you display a document in Print Preview. To switch to Edit mode, click the Magnifier button.

⌘-8

Toggle the display of all nonprinting characters

Pressing this shortcut is the equivalent of selecting or clearing the All check box in the Nonprinting Characters section of the View tab of the Preferences dialog box (Word | Preferences). Nonprinting characters include spaces, tabs, paragraph marks, optional hyphens, and hidden text.

Control-Shift-C

Close the active pane or remove the document window split

This shortcut is particularly useful for closing the header or footer area after working in it.

⌘-Option-S

Toggle horizontal splitting on the active window

Split the window horizontally into two panes when you need to view two different areas of the same document simultaneously. (Alternatively, open a new window on the document.) You can use a different view in each pane if necessary. For example, you could use Normal view for editing in one pane and Outline view for outlining in the other pane.

You can use the next set of keyboard shortcuts to move from one pane to another.

To remove the split, press ⌘-Option-S again.

F6, Shift-F6

Switch to the other pane

Use these shortcuts to switch from one pane of the active document window to the next pane or the previous pane. These shortcuts work both when you've split the window manually and when you're working in a view that automatically displays another pane—for example, when you have the Footnotes pane open.

Control-F6, Option-F6

Activate the next document window

Use whichever of these shortcuts you find most comfortable. Because these are redundant, you might choose to reassign one of the shortcuts to another window-related command that you find useful—or to a completely unrelated command, if you prefer.

Control-Shift-F6, Option-Shift-F6

Activate the previous document window

As with the next-window shortcuts, use whichever of these triple-key shortcuts you find most comfortable. (If you have only two windows open, you can use the next-window shortcuts to toggle between them—whichever window the focus is currently in, the other window is next.) Again, you might choose to reassign whichever of these shortcuts you don't use to another window-related command.

Navigating Through Documents

If you work with documents that are more than a few pages long, navigating to the appropriate points in them can become a vital part of your work. Word provides several tools and shortcuts for navigating through documents.

Shortcuts for Navigating Through Documents

⌘-F

Display the Find tab of the Find And Replace dialog box

Word's Find feature on the Find tab of the Find And Replace dialog box (Figure 4-1) offers a wide variety of options. You can search simply for text, or for text with specific formatting (which you specify by using the Format drop-down menu), or for formatting without text (for example, you might search for the next instance of a specific style). You can constrain the search to matching case or to finding only whole words rather than matches inside other words. You can also choose between searching the current document, part of the current document, or all open documents.

⌘-Shift-H

Display the Replace tab of the Find And Replace dialog box

Word's Replace feature offers similar functions to the Find feature: you can replace text, text with specific formatting, or just formatting. Use the Find Next button to find the next instance of the search item, and the Replace button to replace the current instance. Use the Replace All button to replace all instances of the search term within the selection (if there is one) or within the active document.

Shift-F4, ⌘-Option-Y

Find the next occurrence of the search item

These shortcuts enable you to repeat your last search without displaying the Find And Replace dialog box. Alternatively, you can click the Next Find/Go To button

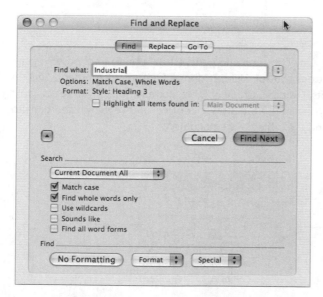

Figure 4-1
Word's Find feature provides a wide range of options for searching for text, formatting, and special characters.

Word

at the bottom of the vertical scroll bar. The disadvantage of using the Next Find/ Go To button is that Word may be set to browse to a different browse object than Find.

⌘-G, F5

Display the Go To tab of the Find And Replace dialog box

The Go To tab of the Find And Replace dialog box (shown here) lets you quickly navigate to pages, bookmarks, and other objects in your documents.

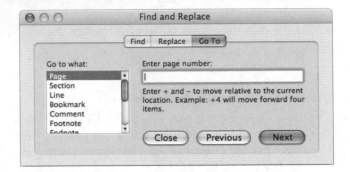

You can also display the Go To tab by double-clicking an area in the status bar that doesn't contain another control.

Double-click in this area to display the Go To tab of the Find And Replace dialog box.

⌘-Page Down

Select the next Browse object

Use the Select Browse Object button and panel (shown here) to choose which object the Browse buttons control: Field, Endnote, Footnote, Comment, Section, Page, Go To, Find, Edits, Heading, Graphic, Table. For example, if you select Table in the Browse panel, you can use the Browse controls and keyboard shortcuts to navigate quickly among the tables in the document.

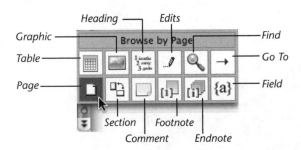

Performing a Find or Replace operation automatically sets the Browse object to Find. So after you've used Find and Replace, you can use ⌘-Page Up and ⌘-Page Down to repeat the Find operation until you change the Browse object. But because you may need to set the Browse object manually, you may find the Shift-F4 and ⌘-Option-Y shortcuts more convenient for accessing the next Find item than the ⌘-Page Down shortcut.

⌘-Page Up

Select the previous Browse object

When the Browse object is set to Find, this shortcut is particularly useful for finding the previous instance of the current search term.

⌘-Shift-F5

Display the Bookmark dialog box

Use bookmarks to assign names to sections of your documents so that you can access them easily either manually or when programming with Visual Basic for Applications (VBA).

Editing Text

If you work with documents at all, you can benefit from the editing shortcuts that Word offers. These range from quickly returning to one of the last three edits made in the document to using the Spike feature for collecting a series of items cut from a document.

Shortcuts for Editing Text

Shift-F5, ⌘-Option-Z

Return to the previous editing point

Word tracks the locations of the last three edits you made to a document. You can return to the last edit by pressing these shortcuts once, the second-last edit by pressing them twice, or the third-last edit by pressing them three times. Pressing a fourth time returns you to the current edit.

>> **Note:** *What Word counts as an "edit" depends not only on the actions you take (for example, typing text or deleting text) but also on the speed at which you take the actions and the intervals between them. So using the Shift-F5 and ⌘-Option-Z shortcuts may not return the insertion point to where you expect; but it's almost always worth trying before other means of navigating to other areas of the document.*

Word

⌘-Y, Option-Return

Repeat the previous action

These shortcuts make Word repeat the previous editing action—for example, applying a style, typing a word or phrase, or inserting an object such as a table. If the editing action isn't what you expected, press ⌘-Z to undo the action immediately.

⌘-Z, F1

Undo the previous action

Press either of these shortcuts to undo the last action you took. Press multiple times to undo multiple actions.

≫ Caution: *The previous action may not be exactly what you think. For example, if you type several words, backspace over a couple of words, and then type a correction, Word registers a single action that consists of typing those words you typed but didn't backspace over. But if you perform the same actions with pauses in between, Word usually considers typing the final words (after the backspacing) to be a separate action.*

Control-⌘-A

Select all

A Select All command selects all the contents of the current object—for example, a document or a text box. If a Select All command selects the wrong object, select the right object and issue the command again.

⌘-F3

Cut the selection and add it to the Spike

The Spike is a special AutoText entry to which you can cut a series of selections to assemble them in order. You then paste the contents of the Spike into the destination. Because the Spike is destructive to the documents you're working in (you can only cut to the Spike—you can't copy to it), few people use it. The best way to use the Spike is to either work on a copy of your source document or save the document, cut the material to the Spike, and then close the document without saving changes.

⌘-Shift-F3

Insert the contents of the Spike

Use this command after assembling content on the Spike as described in the previous entry. Inserting the contents of the Spike into a document clears the Spike.

Formatting Text

Word offers many shortcuts for applying formatting to the text in your documents.

Shortcuts for Formatting Text

⌘-Shift-A

Toggle all caps

All caps capitalizes all letters in the selection but has no effect on nonletter keys (for example, numbers)—unlike pressing Shift and typing.

⌘-Shift-K

Toggle small caps

Small Caps applies small capitals to all letters in the selection.

Shift-F3, ⌘-Option-C

Cycle the case of the selection

This shortcut cycles the case among lowercase, title case (the first letter of each word is capitalized), and uppercase (all letters are capitalized). This shortcut is an alternative to the Format | Change Case command, but that command also offers a Sentence Case option (the first letter of each sentence is capitalized) and a tOGGLE cASE command (Word inverts the capitalization of each letter).

⌘-B, ⌘-Shift-B

Toggle boldface

Both these shortcuts work the same way, but there's no reason to use the ⌘-Shift-B shortcut unless you've reassigned the ⌘-B shortcut. (The ⌘-Shift-B shortcut is there for backward compatibility with older versions of Word.)

Word

⌘-Ⓤ, ⌘-Shift-Ⓤ

Toggle underline

Both these shortcuts work the same way, but there's no reason to use the ⌘-Shift-Ⓤ shortcut (which is there for backward compatibility) unless you've reassigned the ⌘-Ⓤ shortcut.

⌘-Shift-Ⓦ

Toggle word underline

Word underline applies an underscore to each word and to punctuation, but not to the spaces between words. Unlike with the previous two shortcuts, you must press ⌘-Shift-Ⓦ to apply word underline from the keyboard: ⌘-Ⓦ is the shortcut for closing the active window.

⌘-Shift-Ⓓ

Toggle double underlining on the selection

⌘-⑀

Toggle subscript

Subscript decreases the font size of the selected text and lowers it below the baseline of the other characters.

≫ Note: *The Character Spacing tab of the Font dialog box (press* ⌘-Ⓓ *) gives you finer control over subscripts and superscripts.*

⌘-Shift-⑉

Toggle superscript

Superscript decreases the font size of the selected text and raises it above the baseline of the other characters.

⌘-Ⓓ, ⌘-Shift-Ⓕ

Display the Font dialog box

If your hands are on the keyboard, ⌘-Ⓓ is the easiest way of displaying the Font dialog box, but ⌘-Shift-Ⓕ is easier to remember.

Control-Shift-Ⓟ, ⌘-Shift-⑈

Increase the font size in jumps

With this shortcut and the ⌘-Shift-⑈ shortcut, Word uses the font sizes listed in the Font Size drop-down list and the Font dialog box: 8, 9, 10, 11, 12, 14, 16, 18, 20 22, 24, 28, 28, 36, 48, and 72.

⌘-Shift-<

Decrease the font size in jumps

Use this shortcut to quickly decrease the font size to the next size that Word lists.

⌘-]

Increase the font size by one point

Use this shortcut to increase the font size gradually. If you hold down this shortcut, you can wait as Word gradually increases the font size to the size you need.

⌘-[

Decrease the font size by one point

Use this shortcut to decrease the font size gradually rather than in jumps. Again, you can hold down this shortcut and wait as Word gradually decreases the font size.

⌘-Shift-S

Select the Style drop-down list or display the Style dialog box

If the Formatting toolbar is displayed, pressing this shortcut selects the Style drop-down list on the toolbar. If the Formatting toolbar isn't displayed, pressing this shortcut displays the Style dialog box.

⌘-Shift-F

Select the Font drop-down list or display the Font dialog box

If the Formatting toolbar is displayed, pressing this shortcut selects the Font drop-down list on the toolbar. If the Formatting toolbar isn't displayed, pressing this shortcut displays the Font dialog box.

⌘-Option-K

AutoFormat the document

The AutoFormat operation uses the settings you've chosen on the AutoFormat tab of the AutoCorrect Options dialog box (Tools | AutoCorrect).

» Caution: *When you press* ⌘-Option-K, *Word performs the AutoFormat without confirmation. If you pressed the shortcut by mistake, press* F1 *or* ⌘-Z *immediately to undo the AutoFormat.*

Control-Shift-H

Format the selection as hidden text

You can display hidden text by pressing Control-Shift-*, by selecting the Hidden Text check box or the All check box on the View tab of the Preferences

Word

dialog box (Word | Preferences), or by clicking the Show/Hide ¶ button on the Standard toolbar.

⌘-Shift-C

Copy the formatting of the selection

 Pressing this keyboard shortcut is the equivalent of clicking the Format Painter button on the Standard toolbar: it copies the formatting of the selected text or other object to the Clipboard, so that you can paste it to other text (or another object).

⌘-Shift-V

Apply the copied formatting to the selection

After copying formatting using ⌘-Shift-C (or by clicking the Format Painter button), apply the formatting to its destination by using this shortcut or by clicking the Format Painter button.

Formatting Paragraphs

The key to laying out your documents successfully in Word is to apply the correct paragraph formatting by using paragraph styles, direct paragraph formatting, character styles, and direct character formatting. Here's how those four elements work together.

1. The paragraph style defines the overall formatting for the paragraph—everything from the font, font size, and font style to the line spacing and any indentation used.

2. After applying the style, you can apply any direct paragraph formatting needed to modify the style formatting just for this paragraph. For example, you might add more space before or after a particular paragraph.

3. You can then add any character style needed for applying consistent character formatting to individual words or characters in the paragraph. For example, you might use a Bold Italic character style to pick out words or phrases that needed extra emphasis, or apply a Superscript character style to characters that consistently need to be positioned on a higher baseline than other characters.

4. Finally, you can apply any direct character formatting needed to adjust the appearance of individual words or characters in ways that your character styles don't cover. For example, you might need to increase the font size of some characters to make them stand out, but not so many characters to make it worth creating a separate character style.

Shortcuts for Formatting Paragraphs

⌘-Option-M
Display the Paragraph dialog box

The Paragraph dialog box provides one-stop access to most of the commands for formatting paragraphs and is convenient for making multiple adjustments at once to the same paragraph. But when you need to make only one or two adjustments, you can often make them more quickly by using keyboard shortcuts.

⌘-Option-1 to 3
Apply the specified heading level to the selection

⌘-Option-1 applies Heading 1 level, ⌘-Option-2 applies Heading 2 level, and ⌘-Option-3 applies Heading 3 level.

⌘-Shift-L
Apply the List Bullet style to the selection

⌘-Shift-N, Option-Shift-Delete
Apply the Normal style

Word uses the Normal style for all paragraphs that you don't explicitly apply another style to. For example, if you create a new blank document (which is based on the Normal global template), you'll probably find Word starts you off with the Normal style. When you create your own templates, set the starting paragraph to the appropriate style rather than leaving it in Normal style.

⌘-T
Apply or increase the hanging indent

Press this shortcut once to apply the hanging indent. Press it again to increase the hanging indent by one tab stop.

>> **Note:** *The four indentation shortcuts discussed here don't work if you've turned off Word's AutoFormat indentation features.*

⌘-Shift-T
Decrease or remove the hanging indent

Press this shortcut once to decrease the hanging indent by one tab. When the indent is hanging by a single tab, press this shortcut to remove the indent.

Word

Control - Shift - M

Increase the left indent

Each press of this shortcut increases the left indent by a single tab.

⌘ - Shift - M

Decrease the left indent

Each press of this shortcut decreases the left indent by a single tab.

⌘ - Option - Q

Apply the default paragraph format of the current style

Use this shortcut to remove extra formatting that you've applied to a paragraph. For example, if you've applied direct formatting (such as bold or italic) or character styles, use this shortcut to remove them quickly and restore the paragraph's formatting to that of its paragraph style.

Control - Spacebar , Control - Shift - Z

Reset the formatting of the current word or selection

Use this shortcut to quickly remove direct formatting that you've applied to text.

⌘ - J

Apply justified alignment to the paragraph

Applying justified alignment to (or "justifying") a paragraph aligns the left end of its lines with the left margin and the right end of its lines with the right margin. The last line isn't aligned with the right margin unless it happens to reach the margin anyway.

⌘ - 0

Add or remove extra spacing on selected paragraphs

If the selected paragraphs have no extra space, press this shortcut to set the Before measurement to 12 points (in other words, add 12 points before the paragraph). If the selected paragraphs do have extra space, press this shortcut to remove the space.

⌘ - 1

Apply single line spacing

This shortcut (and the next two shortcuts) are useful for quickly changing the line spacing of the active paragraph or the selected paragraphs. But if you find yourself using them frequently, you should probably change the line spacing in the styles you're using.

⌘-⑤

Apply 1.5 line spacing

⌘-②

Apply double line spacing

Working with Fields

Fields can be one of the most confusing parts of a Word document. A *field* is a code that represents information that's stored somewhere else—either somewhere else in the same document (for example, a field that returns the contents of a bookmark), on your computer, or on a networked computer—or generated automatically (for example, a field that returns the date or the number of pages in the document).

When you insert a field in a document, Word typically displays the *field result* (the information the field returns) rather than the *field code* (text that details the information the field references). For example, the date field code {**DATE \ a "dddd, MMMM dd, yyyy" *MERGEFORMAT**} might display the field result **Thursday, April 01, 2004**. You can toggle a field between displaying the field result and the field code.

To make sure a document contains the latest information available, you need to update the fields it contains. In other cases, you'll need to lock the fields in a document to prevent them from changing. When you want to freeze the current information in the fields and prevent it from changing again (even if its source is updated), you can unlink the fields from their sources.

Shortcuts for Working with Fields

Control-Shift-P

Insert a page-number field at the insertion point

This shortcut is faster in most cases than using the Field dialog box (Insert | Field) to insert the page number. However, if you're working in the header and footer areas, you may find it easier to click the Insert Page Number button on the Header And Footer toolbar. The Header And Footer toolbar also includes the Insert Number Of Pages button, which lets you easily create "Page 1 of 10"-style numbering.

Insert Page Number   *Insert Number Of Pages*

Control -Shift - D
Insert a date field in the first date format at the insertion point

The first date format is the date format that appears at the top of the Available Formats list box in the Date And Time dialog box (Insert | Date And Time.)

Control -Shift - T
Insert a time field in the first time format at the insertion point

The first time format is the first time format that appears in the Available Formats list box in the Date And Time dialog box (Insert | Date And Time.)

Option - F9
Toggle between field codes and field results

This shortcut is the quickest way to toggle the display of field codes in the active document. You can also toggle the display of field codes by choosing Edit | Preferences, selecting or clearing the Field Codes check box in the Show area of the View tab of the Preferences dialog box, and then clicking the OK button.

⌘ - 3 , ⌘ - F11
Lock the fields in the current selection

Fields that you lock can't be changed until you unlock them.

⌘ - 4 , ⌘ - Shift - F11
Unlock the fields in the current selection

Unlock locked fields when you need to be able to update them again.

F9 , ⌘ - Option - Shift - U
Update the fields in the selection

To update all the fields in a document, press ⌘ - A to select all, and then press this shortcut.

⌘ - 6 , ⌘ - Shift - F9
Unlink the fields in the current selection

Select the fields you want to unlink before pressing either of these shortcuts. To unlink all the fields in the active document, press ⌘ - A to select the document, and then press one of these shortcuts.

DR | ‖‖‖‖‖‖ ‖ ‖‖ ‖‖‖‖ ‖ ‖ ‖‖

⌘-Shift-F7

Copy the modifications in a linked object back to its source file

This shortcut works only for fields that contain objects derived from, and still linked to, sources in other files.

Option-Shift-F9

"Click" the selected field

Press this shortcut to perform a click action on the selected field.

⌘-F9

Insert the braces for a field

When you want to construct a field by typing it manually rather than by using the Field dialog box (Insert | Field), press ⌘-F9 to insert the brace characters— {}—and then type the field inside them.

> ≫ **Note:** *The brace characters Word uses for fields are different from the brace characters you can type using the keyboard. To create a field manually, you must enter the brace characters by using this shortcut rather than by typing them.*

⌘-Option-Shift-L

Insert a List Numbered field

For example, press this shortcut once to enter **1)** to start a list. Press this shortcut twice to enter **1)a).**

> ≫ **Note:** *If you're using Jaguar, you can use the keyboard shortcuts F11 (to select the next field) and Shift-F11 (to select the previous field). Panther uses F11 for Exposé's Show the Desktop feature, and pressing Shift with F11 simply slows down the animation. But if you reassign the desktop keyboard shortcut on the Exposé sheet of System Preferences ([Apple] | System Preferences), you can use these field-navigation shortcuts in Word on Panther too. Similarly, Exposé uses F9 to display all applications; so if you want to use Shift-F9 to toggle the display of a selected field, you'll need to reassign F9 in Exposé.*

F11

Select the next field

See the previous Note for limitations on this shortcut.

Shift-F11

Select the previous field

See the previous Note for limitations on this shortcut.

Shift-F9

Toggle field codes and field results

Press this shortcut to toggle the display of the selected field or fields between field codes and field results. But see the previous Note for limitations on this shortcut.

Working with Outlines

Word's Outline view is a powerful tool for creating, organizing, and editing long or complex documents. Most users use the mouse extensively when working in Outline view, but if you're creating an outline, using the keyboard tends to be much faster.

Shortcuts for Working with Outlines

⌘-Option-O

Apply Outline view

Control-Shift-1 to 9

Display Outline Level 1–9

Press Control-Shift and the appropriate number for the number of heading levels you want to display. For example, press Control-Shift-1 to display Outline Level 1 paragraphs only, Control-Shift-2 to display up to Outline Level 2 paragraphs, and Control-Shift-9 to display up to Outline Level 9 paragraphs.

Control-_ , Control-Shift--

Collapse the lowest subtext in the selection

On a typical keyboard, these shortcuts are the same, because the underscore is the shifted version of the hyphen key. Select the heading you want to affect, hold down Control-Shift, and press the hyphen key repeatedly to collapse each lowest level of the selection in turn.

Control-Shift-+

Expand the next level of subtext in the selection

Select the heading you want to affect, hold down Control-Shift, and press the plus key once for each outline level you want to expand.

[Control]-[Shift]-[↓]

Move the selection down one item in the outline

Select one or more contiguous items, and then press this shortcut to move the selection down one displayed item at a time. (For example, if you have expanded the section of the outline you're working in to show Level 3 items, each press of this shortcut moves the selection down one Level 3 item, one Level 2 item, or one Level 1 item—whichever is next in the displayed outline.)

This shortcut and the next tend to be much easier than dragging items with the mouse because they remove the chance of your changing the outline level of the item at the same time by dragging it to the left or the right.

[Control]-[Shift]-[↑]

Move the selection up one item in the outline

Select one or more contiguous items, and then press this shortcut to move the selection up one displayed item at a time. (See the previous description for more details.)

[Control]-[Shift]-[L]

Toggle the outline between displaying the first line of each paragraph and the full text of each paragraph

 This shortcut is the equivalent of clicking the Show First Line Only button on the Outlining toolbar.

[Control]-[Shift]-[A]

Toggle the display of all headings and body text

 This shortcut is the equivalent of selecting the Show All Headings button on the Outlining toolbar.

[Control]-[Shift]-[←], [Shift]-[Tab]

Promote the selection by one heading level

 This shortcut is the equivalent of clicking the Promote button.

[Control]-[Shift]-[→], [Tab]

Demote the selection by one heading level

 This shortcut is the equivalent of clicking the Demote button.

Inserting Items

Word offers keyboard shortcuts for inserting various different items, ranging from AutoText entries to time fields, into your documents.

Shortcuts for Inserting Items

⌘-Option-V

Insert an AutoText entry

See "Using AutoText," at the end of this chapter, for a discussion of what AutoText is, what you can do with it, and how to do it.

⌘-Return

Insert a section break at the insertion point

⌘-Shift-Return, ⌘-Shift-R

Insert a column break at the insertion point

⌘-Option-A

Insert an annotation at the insertion point

Word displays the Comments pane so that you can insert the comment. Press Control-Shift-C to close the Comments pane after entering the comment.

⌘-Option-E

Insert an endnote at the insertion point

In Normal view, Word displays the Endnotes pane if it's not already displayed.

⌘-Option-F

Insert a footnote at the insertion point

In Normal view, Word displays the Footnotes pane if it's not already displayed.

Checking Your Documents

Word includes shortcuts for accessing its tools for checking the text of your documents and tracking changes to them.

....
Shortcuts for Checking Your Documents

Run the Spelling and Grammar Checker

Word's default settings are to check grammar in your documents while checking the spelling. Provided that the dictionary spellings are correct, spelling is eminently suitable for checking by computer, because any particular word is spelled either correctly or incorrectly; but grammar is much less suited to checking by computer, because it is complex and full of subtleties. So while you will probably benefit from using the Spelling Checker, you may well want to turn off the Grammar Checker. To do so, choose Word | Preferences, click the Spelling And Grammar item in the list box in the Properties dialog box, clear the Check Grammar With Spelling check box and the Check Grammar As You Type check box, and then click the OK button.

Option-F7

Find the next spelling error

This shortcut is great for quickly moving from one apparent spelling error to the next in a document.

⌘-Shift-E

Toggle Track Changes on and off

This shortcut is an alternative to clicking the TRK indicator in the status bar to toggle the Track Changes setting.

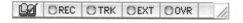

Option-Shift-F7

Look up the selected word in the Thesaurus

Working with Tables

Word offers only a handful of keyboard shortcuts for working with tables, but most of them are well worth knowing.

Shortcuts for Working with Tables

[Tab]

Move to the next cell and select its contents

Press [Tab] to move to the next cell, automatically selecting its contents. (After pressing [Tab], press [←] to deselect the selection and move the insertion point to the beginning of the cell, or press [→] to deselect the selection and move the insertion point to the end of the cell.)

If the current cell is the last cell in the table, pressing [Tab] adds a new row to the table after the current last row and selects the first cell in the new row.

[Shift]-[Tab]

Move to the previous cell and select its contents

Press [Shift]-[Tab] to move to the previous cell, automatically selecting its contents. (After pressing [Shift]-[Tab], press [←] to deselect the selection and move the insertion point to the beginning of the cell, or press [→] to deselect the selection and move the insertion point to the end of the cell.)

[⌘]-[Option]-[T]

Select all of the current table

Use this shortcut when you need to manipulate all of a table. You can also use it when you need to move quickly to the beginning or end of the table: select all the table; then press [←] to deselect the selection and move the insertion point to the beginning of the table or [→] to deselect the selection and move the insertion point to the end of the table.

[⌘]-[Shift]-[Return]

Split the table at the insertion point

Click to place the insertion point at the beginning of the row at which you want to split the table, and then press this shortcut. This shortcut is the equivalent of the Table | Split Table command.

≫ Tip: *Use the [⌘]-[Shift]-[Return] shortcut (or the Split Table command) when a document has a table as its first item, and you need to insert paragraphs above the table.*

⌘-Control-V

Insert a row above the active row

To insert multiple rows, select cells in the corresponding number of rows before pressing this shortcut. (For example, select cells in three rows to insert three new rows.)

⌘-Control-X

Delete the active row

⌘-Option-U

Update autoformatting on the selected table

You may need to update the autoformatting on a table after you add or delete rows, columns, or cells.

Performing Mail Merge

Word supports the following keyboard shortcuts for performing common mail-merge operations. Most of these shortcuts work only after you've created a merge document and linked it to a data source.

Shortcuts for Performing Mail Merge

Control-Shift-F

Display the Insert Merge Field dialog box

Use the Insert Merge Field dialog box (shown here) to insert a merge field in the mail-merge document.

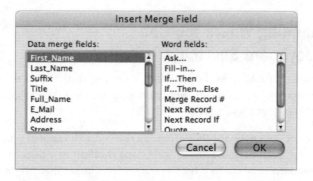

Word

>> **Note:** *You can also insert merge fields (and perform most other merge operations) by using the Data Merge Manager (Tools | Data Merge Manager).*

Display the Checking And Reporting Errors dialog box

In the Checking And Reporting Errors dialog box (shown here), select the type of check you want to perform, and then click the OK button.

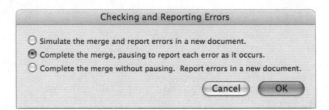

Open a mail-merge data source

Control - Shift - N

Merge the records to a new document

Customizing Word to Add Your Shortcuts

As you've seen so far in this chapter, Word comes with an impressive number of keyboard shortcuts already built in. But if you use Word extensively, you'll more than likely want to add keyboard shortcuts of your own or customize the built-in keyboard shortcuts. Word offers great flexibility here as well.

Understanding Where You Can Create Keyboard Shortcuts

You can create customized keyboard shortcuts in any document, any template, or in the Normal global template. (Normal is loaded all the time Word is running.) Here's how these three layers work:

- **Document**   A keyboard shortcut you create in a document works only when that document is active. A keyboard shortcut in a document overrides any keyboard shortcut that uses the same keys in the document's template or in the Normal template.

- **Template**   A keyboard shortcut you create in a template works when a document attached to that template is open or when the template itself is open. (Usually, you don't open a template directly except when you need to make changes to its contents. Instead, you work with documents based on the template.) The keyboard shortcut overrides any keyboard shortcut that uses the same keys in the Normal template but can itself be overridden by a keyboard shortcut in the attached document.

- **Normal template** A keyboard shortcut you create in the Normal template works any time that Word is running, except when a keyboard shortcut in the active document or the template attached to the active document overrides it.

>> Caution: *Shortcuts already used by Mac OS X aren't available for assignment. For example,* ⌘-Option-D *toggles hiding on the Dock. You can't assign this shortcut to a Word command.*

Being able to create keyboard shortcuts in three different layers gives you great flexibility in creating shortcuts. But it also means that when you create a shortcut, you must make sure you're putting it in the right place:

- If you want your shortcuts to be available whenever you're using Word, create them in the Normal template.

- If you need a shortcut only in documents based on a particular template, create it in that template.

- If you need a shortcut only in a particular document, create it in that document.

Creating New Keyboard Shortcuts

To create a new keyboard shortcut in Word, follow these steps:

1. Choose Tools | Customize to display the Customize dialog box.

2. Click the Keyboard button on any of the three tabs to display the Customize Keyboard dialog box. To enable you to see all the components of the Customize Keyboard dialog box, Figure 4-2 shows the dialog box with an assignment under way.

3. In the Save Changes In drop-down list, select the document or template to which you want to apply the keyboard shortcut.

4. In the Categories list box, select the category of item for which you want to create or change the keyboard shortcut. The list box to the right of the Categories list box changes its name to match the category you select.

   - Each of the eight menu categories (File, Edit, View, Insert, Format, Tools, Table, and Window and Help) lists the commands associated with that menu. The more often used commands appear on the menus, while the less used commands don't appear. For example, the FilePrint command appears on the File menu as the Print command, while the FileConfirmConversions command doesn't appear.

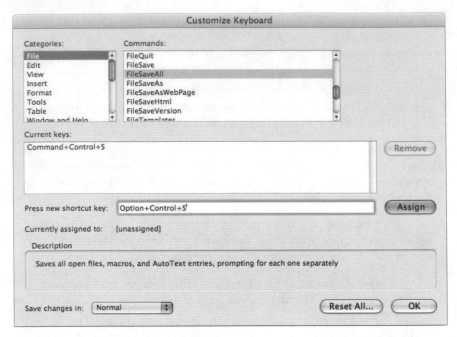

Figure 4-2   *The Customize Keyboard dialog box lets you assign a keyboard shortcut to almost any command, macro, font, AutoText entry, style, or common symbol.*

- The Drawing category lists the commands associated with the Drawing toolbar.

- The Borders category lists the commands associated with the border buttons on the Tables And Borders toolbar.

- The Mail Merge category lists the commands associated with the Data Merge Manager (Tools | Data Merge Manager).

- The All Commands category lists the full list of Word commands. Because there are so many commands, this list is awkward to use, so you'll probably want to use it only when you can't remember which menu a command is associated with.

- The Macros category lists all the macros available in the active document and templates.

- The Fonts category lists the fonts installed on Mac OS X.

- The AutoText category lists the AutoText entries defined in Word.

- The Styles category lists the styles available in the active document and templates.

- The Common Symbols category lists frequently used symbols (such as em dashes, ® and © marks, and paragraph marks).

5. In the Commands list box, select the command for which you want to create or change a keyboard shortcut. Word displays any existing keyboard shortcut for the command in the Current Keys list box.

6. Press ⌘-N or click in the Press New Shortcut Key text box to put the focus there.

7. Press the keyboard shortcut you want to assign. If this shortcut is currently assigned to another command, Word displays the Currently Assigned To line listing the command, so that you'll know which existing shortcut you're about to overwrite. Choose a different keyboard shortcut if necessary.

8. Click the Assign button to assign the keyboard shortcut to the command.

9. Assign further keyboard shortcuts as necessary.

10. Click the Close button to close the Customize Keyboard dialog box.

11. Click the Close button to close the Customize dialog box.

After adding keyboard shortcuts, save the document or template, as discussed in "Saving Your Changes," a little later in this chapter.

Removing and Resetting Keyboard Shortcuts

To remove a keyboard shortcut, display the Customize Keyboard dialog box, specify which document or template you want to affect, and select the command so that Word displays the current keyboard shortcut. Select the shortcut in the Current Keys list box, and then click the Remove button.

To reset all keyboard shortcuts in the specified document or template to their default settings, click the Reset All button, and then click the Yes button in the confirmation dialog box:

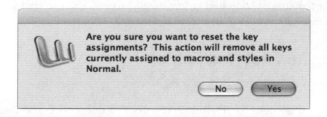

Are you sure you want to reset the key assignments? This action will remove all keys currently assigned to macros and styles in Normal.

No   Yes

» *Note:* *The Reset All button isn't available until the document or template contains customized keyboard shortcuts.*

After removing or resetting keyboard shortcuts, save the document or template, as described next.

Saving Your Changes

After customizing keyboard shortcuts in a document, template, or the Normal template, immediately save the file you customized to avoid losing the customization should Word or Mac OS X crash:

- To save the document, issue a Save command by pressing ⌘-⑤, clicking the Save button, or choosing File | Save as usual.

- To save the template attached to the document, issue a Save command for the document. Word then prompts you to save changes to the document template. Click the Yes button.

- To save changes to the Normal template, hold down ⑤ᴴⁱᶠᵗ as you click the File menu to display the menu with the Save All command in place of the Save command. Then choose the Save All item. Word saves the active document and saves the Normal template. (If you've selected the Prompt To Save Normal Template check box on the Save tab of the Preferences dialog box, Word prompts you to save changes to the Normal template. Click the Yes button.)

Using AutoText

As you saw in Chapter 3, AutoCorrect can help you enter text items quickly and automatically in any of the Office applications. In Word, you can create formatted AutoCorrect entries as well, which can contain not only formatted text but also graphics.

Word also lets you create AutoText entries for inserting boilerplate text and graphics in your documents. AutoText entries are very similar to AutoCorrect entries, but they're not triggered automatically, so you can use standard words in their names.

Creating New AutoText Entries

To create an AutoText entry, follow these steps:

1. Create the contents of the AutoText entry in a document, and then select the material for the entry.

2. Press ⌥Option⌥-⌥F3⌥ (or click the New button on the AutoText toolbar) to display the Create AutoText dialog box:

3. In the Please Name Your AutoText Entry text box, edit the default name that Word suggests. (The default name for AutoText entries you create this way consists of the first two words of the text—assuming the text has at least two words.)

4. Click the OK button to close the Create AutoText dialog box and create the AutoText entry.

Deleting AutoText Entries

To delete an AutoText entry, display the AutoText tab of the AutoCorrect dialog box (Tools | AutoCorrect). Figure 4-3 shows the AutoText tab. Select the entry and click the Delete button.

From the AutoText tab of the AutoCorrect dialog box, you can also create an AutoText entry from the current selection by clicking the Add button, but it's usually easier to use the Create AutoText dialog box, as described a moment ago.

The most important option on the AutoText tab is the Show AutoComplete Tip For AutoText, Contacts, And Dates check box, which controls whether Word displays a ScreenTip showing an available AutoText entry, contact name, or date when you've typed enough letters to identify it. Clear this check box if you prefer to trigger your AutoText entries manually.

The Preview box helps you identify an AutoText entry that you can't identify by its name. You can then click the Insert button to insert the entry at the insertion point.

Entering AutoText Entries

The standard way to enter an AutoText entry is to use the AutoComplete feature. When Word notices that you've typed the first few characters in an AutoText

Word

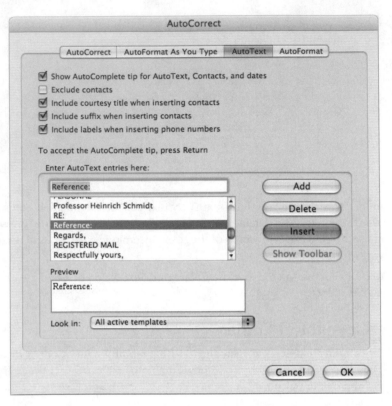

Figure 4-3   *Use the AutoText tab of the AutoCorrect dialog box to delete AutoText entries.*

entry's name, it displays a ScreenTip showing the first few words of the AutoText entry so that you can identify it:

You can press Tab to enter the AutoText entry and continue typing in the same paragraph, or press Return to enter the AutoText entry and start a new paragraph.

If you prefer not to use AutoComplete, you can enter an AutoText entry by typing enough letters to identify it, and then pressing Option-F3. (If Word beeps when you press Option-F3, you haven't typed enough letters to uniquely identify the AutoText entry.)

You can also insert AutoText entries by using the Insert | AutoText submenu or the drop-down menu button on the AutoText toolbar.

Moving AutoText Entries from One Template to Another

AutoText entries are stored in templates. By default, Word stores all your AutoText entries in the Normal template, the global template that's loaded whenever you start Word. But you can copy or move AutoText entries from one template to another if necessary. Having all your AutoText entries in the Normal template is convenient because it means they're always available when you're working in Word, no matter which template the active document is attached to. But if your AutoText entries are large (for example, if they contain graphics), the Normal template will grow to a large file size, which can make Word run more slowly. In this case, it's a good idea to move any AutoText entries that apply only to a certain template to that template so that they're not slowing down Word.

You'll also need to store AutoText entries in their own templates if you want to make different AutoText entries available for different templates. When you do this, the AutoText entries in the template to which the active document is attached take precedence over the AutoText entries in the Normal template.

To copy or move AutoText entries from one template to another, follow these steps:

1. Choose Tools | Templates And Add-Ins to display the Templates And Add-Ins dialog box.

2. Click the Organizer button to display the Organizer dialog box.

3. Click the AutoText tab to display it:

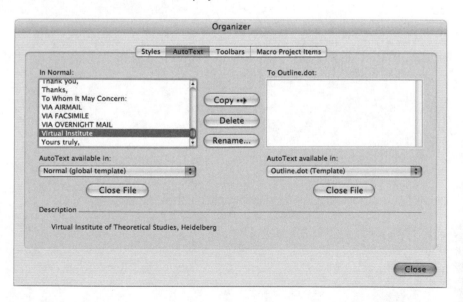

4. If necessary, use the Close File button and the resulting Open File button on each side of the AutoText tab to open the templates you want to work with.

5. In the list box for the source template, select the AutoText entry.

6. Click the Copy button to copy it to the other template.

7. If you want to remove the AutoText entry from the source template, click the Delete button.

8. After copying or moving all the AutoText entries you want to affect, click the Close button to close the Organizer dialog box.

9. Save both the templates involved.

Excel Keyboard Shortcuts

Excel supports a good variety of keyboard shortcuts that can save you a lot of time and hand movement. If you work with the keyboard shortcuts a little, you'll quickly learn which ones benefit you most in your day-to-day work. Some are natural candidates for everyday use, while others are more esoteric.

How much you use the keyboard in Excel is likely to depend on the tasks you're performing. For example, if you need to manipulate elements in a chart, you'll probably find that you use the mouse more than the keyboard. On the other hand, if you spend most of your time building worksheets and entering and editing data, you may be able to send your mouse off for a cup of coffee, or even lunch, without noticing its absence.

If you find using the keyboard handy, you can customize some of Excel's existing keyboard shortcuts and add custom shortcuts of your own. "Customizing Excel to Add Your Shortcuts," at the end of this chapter, shows you how to do so.

Excel's Built-in Keyboard Shortcuts

Excel includes many built-in keyboard shortcuts. This section presents them broken into subsections by type, starting with the differences worth noting about Excel's implementation of the shared Office keyboard shortcuts.

Notes on the Standard Shortcuts

Excel supports the standard Office keyboard shortcuts discussed in "Shared Keyboard Shortcuts" in Chapter 3. The following exceptions are worth noting.

Shortcuts for Creating a New Default Workbook

⌘-N

Create a new default workbook

The new default workbook uses Excel's default settings for font, cell height and width, alignment, and so on. You can customize these default settings for new workbooks by creating a workbook template named Workbook in the Microsoft Office X/Office/Startup/Excel folder or in the alternate startup folder specified in the Alternate Startup File Location text box on the General tab of the Preferences dialog box (press ⌘-, or choose Excel | Preferences). Open the Workbook template and change the settings in it to suit your preferences.

Shortcuts for Opening and Saving Files

Excel offers two extra F12 key shortcuts for opening and saving files.

Control-F12

Display the Open dialog box

In Excel, you can press Control-F12 as well as ⌘-O to display the Open dialog box for opening a file.

Shift-F12

Save the active file

In Excel, you can press Shift-F12 instead of ⌘-S to issue a Save command. Excel also uses the standard F12 shortcut for issuing a Save As command.

Shortcuts for Printing a File

Excel offers an extra F12 shortcut for printing a file.

Control-Shift-F12

Display the Print dialog box

In Excel, you can press Control-Shift-F12 as well as ⌘-P to display the Print dialog box. Most people find ⌘-P much easier, but you might choose to be the exception.

Shortcuts for Working with Find

Excel supports the following extra shortcuts for working with its Find feature.

Shift-F5

Display the Find dialog box

You can use Shift-F5 instead of ⌘-F to display the Find dialog box.

⌘-G, Shift-F4

Find the next instance of the search term

After performing a Find operation and closing the Find And Replace dialog box, you can find the next instance of the last search term without displaying the Find And Replace dialog box by pressing ⌘-G or Shift-F4.

Shortcuts for Working with Windows

Excel supports the following extra shortcuts for working with windows.

Control-F10

Toggle the window between maximized and nonmaximized states

F6

Activate the next pane

Use this shortcut to switch from one pane of a split workbook window to the other pane.

Shift-F6

Activate the previous pane

Use this shortcut to switch from one pane of a split workbook window to the other pane.

Control-F6

Activate the next workbook window

Control-Shift-F6

Activate the previous workbook window

Navigating in Worksheets

Unless your workbooks consist of a single worksheet with only a few cells on it, you'll spend a fair amount of time navigating your worksheets in Excel. Keyboard shortcuts can save you a large amount of scrolling and clicking with the mouse.

Shortcuts for Navigating in Worksheets

←, →, ↑, ↓

Move the active cell left or right one column, or up or down one row

Use the arrow keys for basic navigation. For example, press → to move the active cell highlight to the cell to the right of the current active cell. Hold down the arrow key to move through multiple cells.

Control-.

Move clockwise to the next corner of the selection

Shift-F11

Insert a new default worksheet in the active workbook

>> **Note:** *If you're using Jaguar, you can use* Shift-F11 *to insert a new default worksheet in a workbook. Panther uses* F11 *for Exposé's Show The Desktop feature, and pressing* Shift *with* F11 *slows down the animation. But if you reassign the Desktop keyboard shortcut on the Exposé sheet of System Preferences (| System Preferences), you can use this shortcut in Excel on Panther too.*

Control-Tab

Display the next workbook or workbook window

Press this shortcut to display the next workbook. If a workbook has two or more windows open, Excel displays each window in its turn.

Control-Shift-Tab

Display the previous workbook or workbook window

Press this shortcut to display the next workbook. If a workbook has two or more windows open, Excel displays each window in its turn.

Control-Page Down

Move to the next worksheet

Control-Page Up

Move to the previous worksheet

Control-Shift-Page Down

Select the current worksheet and the next worksheet

Control-Shift-Page Up

Select the current worksheet and the previous worksheet

Control-←, Control-→, Control-↑, Control-↓

Move to the specified edge of the data region

The *data region* is the area of the active worksheet that contains the active cell and has cells that contain data. The data region extends up from the active cell to the nearest blank row above and below, and to the nearest blank column to the left and right. For example, if a worksheet contains entries from cell D8 through K23, the data region starts at cell D8 and extends to row 23 and column K. Pressing [Control]-[→] moves the active cell to column K in the active row. Pressing [Control]-[↓] moves the active cell to row 23 in the active column. Pressing [Control]-[←] returns the active cell to column D, and pressing [Control]-[↑] returns the active cell to row 8.

[Home]

Move to the first cell in the active row

Use this keyboard shortcut to move the active cell from the far reaches of the worksheet to the first column. This keyboard shortcut is especially useful when you need to check row headings that you don't have displayed.

[Control]-[Home]

Move to the first cell in the worksheet

[Control]-[End]

Move to the last used cell in the worksheet

This shortcut moves the active cell to the last cell *ever* used in the worksheet, which may be further down or across the worksheet than the last cell that currently contains data.

[Page Down]

Move down one screen

[Page Up]

Move up one screen

[Option]-[Page Down]

Move to the right by one screen

[Option]-[Page Up]

Move to the left by one screen

[Control]-[Delete]

Display the active cell

If the active cell isn't displayed in the window, Excel scrolls the workbook so that the active cell is displayed.

Shift - Delete

Reduce the selection to the active cell

If the active cell isn't displayed in the window, Excel scrolls the workbook so that the active cell is displayed.

Control - G , F5

Display the Go To dialog box

The Go To dialog box (shown on the left here) lets you quickly access the named ranges in the active worksheet. You can also press ⌘-S from the Go To dialog box to display the Go To Special dialog box (shown on the right here), which lets you access cells that meet specific criteria.

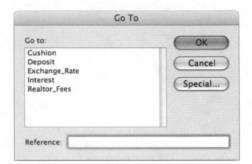
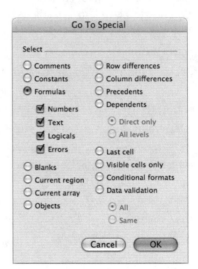

Selecting Cells, Rows, and Columns

To select cells with the mouse, you simply click and drag. Alternatively, click to select the first cell, hold down Shift, and then click the last cell to select the range in between. You can also select cells, rows, and columns with the keyboard by using the following keyboard shortcuts.

Shortcuts for Selecting Cells, Rows, and Columns

Shift - ← , Shift - → , Shift - ↑ , Shift - ↓

Extend the selection in the direction of the arrow key

Hold down Shift and use the arrow keys to extend the selection by as many rows and columns as necessary.

» Note: *You can also use* Shift *and the arrow keys to reduce an existing selection.*

Control - Spacebar
Select the current column or columns

If the selection consists of only the active cell, pressing Control - Spacebar selects only the active column. If the selection consists of cells in multiple columns, pressing Control - Spacebar selects all those columns.

Shift - Spacebar
Select the current row

If the selection consists of only the active cell, pressing Shift - Spacebar selects only the active row. If the selection consists of cells in multiple rows, pressing Shift - Spacebar selects all those rows.

⌘ - A
Select all cells on the current worksheet

Control - Shift - Spacebar
Select all the objects on the current worksheet while retaining the current selection

F8
Toggle Extend mode on and off

Press F8 to turn on Extend mode, and then use the arrow keys and other navigation keys without Shift to select a range. Excel displays EXT on the status bar when Extend mode is on. Press F8 again to turn off Extend mode.

Shift - F8
Toggle Add mode on and off

Turn on Add mode so that you can add another range of cells to the existing selection. Press Shift - F8, and then use the arrow keys and other navigation keys without Shift to select each further range as necessary. Excel displays ADD on the status bar when Add mode is on. Press Shift - F8 again to turn off Add mode.

Control - Shift - ←, Control - Shift - →, Control - Shift - ↑, Control - Shift - ↓
Extend the selection to the first or last cell in the data area

The *data area* is a block of cells containing entries. The end of the data area is defined by a blank column at the left or right, and by a blank row at the top or bottom. Control - Shift - ↑ and Control - Shift - ↓ extend the selection to the first or last row in the data area. Control - Shift - ← and Control - Shift - → extend the selection to the first or last column in the data area. For example, press Control - Shift - → to extend the selection to the last column used in the data area for the row containing the active cell.

Shift-Home
  Extend the selection to the first cell in the row

Control-Shift-Home
  Extend the selection to the first cell in the worksheet

Control-Shift-End
  Extend the selection to the last cell used on the worksheet

  The last cell used is the last cell that has ever contained an entry. It may not currently contain an entry.

End-Shift-←, End-Shift-→, End-Shift-↑, End-Shift-↓
  Extend the selection to the last cell with contents in the active column or row

End-Shift-Home
  Extend the selection to the last cell with contents on the worksheet

End-Shift-Return
  Extend the selection to the last cell in the active row

Shift-Page Down
  Extend the selection downward by one screen

Shift-Page Up
  Extend the selection upward by one screen

Selecting Cells That Match Criteria

Beyond the shortcuts for general selection discussed in the previous section, Excel offers shortcuts for more specialized selection—for example, selecting the cells referenced by a formula, or selecting cells in a row or column whose value is different from the value in the active cell.

Shortcuts for Selecting Cells That Match Criteria

Control-Shift-*
  Select the data area

  The data area is a block of cells containing entries. The end of the data area is defined by a blank column at the left or right, and by a blank row at the top or bottom.

Control-/

Select the array that the active cell is in

Control-\

Select nonmatching cells in the active row

This shortcut selects cells in the active row whose values don't match the value in the active cell. Position the active cell in the appropriate row before pressing this shortcut.

Control-Shift-|

Select nonmatching cells in the active column

This shortcut (which uses the vertical bar, | , rather than the letter *I*) selects cells in the active column whose values don't match the value in the active cell. Position the active cell in the appropriate column before pressing this shortcut.

⌘-Shift-O

Select all cells that have comments attached

This shortcut uses the letter *O*, not zero.

⌘-Shift-Z

Select only the visible cells in the current selection

This shortcut is useful when the selected area contains hidden rows or columns that you don't want to include when copying the contents of the selected area. (If you select the whole area, Excel includes any hidden rows or columns. These rows and columns appear when you paste the data.)

Control-[

Select cells directly referenced by formulas in the active cell

Control-]

Select cells that contain formulas directly referencing the active cell

Control-{

Select cells directly or indirectly referenced by formulas in the active cell

Control-}

Select cells that contain formulas directly or indirectly referencing the active cell

Entering and Editing Data

Excel provides the following keyboard shortcuts for entering data in your worksheets and editing the existing entries in cells. To start entering data in a blank cell, simply select the cell and type the entry.

Shortcuts for Entering and Editing Data

Control - U

Switch the active cell into Edit mode

To edit the existing contents of a cell, select it and press Control - U. Excel places the insertion point at the end of the cell's existing contents.

> **» Note:** *If the Edit Directly In Cell check box on the Edit tab of the Preferences dialog box is cleared, pressing Control - U activates the Formula bar instead.*

Return

Enter the entry in the cell and select the next cell

By default, when you press Return, Excel selects the next cell below the active cell. You can change the direction of the next cell (up, down, left, or right), or turn off the movement, by using the Move Selection After Return check box and Direction drop-down list on the Edit tab of the Preferences dialog box (press ⌘ - , or choose Excel | Preferences).

Esc

Cancel editing in the active cell

Canceling editing loses any changes you've made to the cell's contents.

Shift - Return

Enter the entry in the cell and select the next cell in the opposite direction

Press Shift - Enter to select the cell in the opposite direction from that specified in the Direction drop-down list on the Edit tab of the Preferences dialog box.

Tab

Enter the entry in the cell and select the next cell to the right

> **» Note:** *On a protected worksheet, pressing Tab moves the active cell to the next unprotected cell. Pressing Shift - Tab moves the active cell to the previous unprotected cell.*

Shift - Tab

Enter the entry in the cell and select the next cell to the left

Excel

Control - Return

Fill the selected range with the entry

Select the range of cells you want to affect, type the entry, and press Control - Return to enter it in all the cells simultaneously.

Control - Option - Return

Start a new line in the active cell

Control - D

Fill down

Fill the selected cells beneath the active cell with the contents of the active cell.

Control - R

Fill right

Fill the selected cells to the right of the active cell with the contents of the active cell.

Control - Shift - :

Enter the time in the active cell

Control - ;

Enter the date in the active cell

Control - F3

Display the Define Name dialog box

Use the Define Name dialog box (shown here) to add and delete range names.

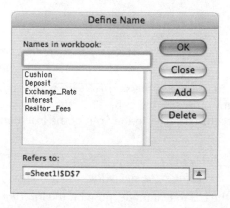

[Control]-[Shift]-[F3]

Display the Create Names dialog box

Use the Create Names dialog box (shown here) to create names from row labels
and column labels.

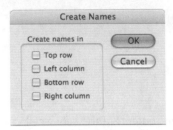

[Option]-[↓]

Display the AutoComplete drop-down list

The AutoComplete drop-down list shows the entries in
the column available for reuse.

[Shift]-[F2]

Insert a new comment or edit the existing comment

If the active cell has a comment attached to it, Excel opens the comment for
editing. If the active cell has no comment, Excel creates a new comment.

[Delete]

Delete the contents of the active cell or the character to the left of the insertion point

When the cell is not in Edit mode, pressing [Delete] deletes the contents of the
active cell and switches it to Edit mode. When the cell is in Edit mode, pressing
[Delete] deletes the character to the left of the insertion point.

[Forward Delete]

*Clear the contents of the active cell or selection, or delete the character to the right of
the insertion point*

When the cell is not in Edit mode, pressing [Forward Delete] deletes the contents of
the active cell and any other selected cells. When the cell is in Edit mode, pressing
[Forward Delete] deletes the character to the right of the insertion point.

[Control]-[Forward Delete]

Delete from the insertion point to the end of the cell's contents

Press [F2] to switch the cell to Edit mode, position the insertion point after the last
character you want to keep, and then press this shortcut to delete the rest.

Control-6

Cycle object display, placeholder display, and hiding

Press Control-6 to cycle between displaying objects, displaying placeholders for objects, and hiding objects.

Control-7

Toggle the display of the Standard toolbar

Displaying and hiding the Standard toolbar this way tends to be quicker than displaying and hiding it using the mouse.

Inserting and Deleting Cells

Excel provides keyboard shortcuts for inserting and deleting cells using the keyboard.

Shortcuts for Inserting and Deleting Cells

Control-[-]

Delete the selected cells

If you have one or more cells selected, Excel displays the Delete dialog box (shown here) so that you can specify in which direction to move the remaining cells. You can also choose to delete the row or column. If you press this shortcut with one or more rows or columns selected, Excel deletes the rows or columns without confirmation.

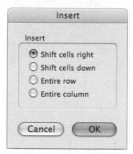

Control-Shift-[+]

Insert cells

Excel displays the Insert dialog box (shown here) so that you can choose whether to move the other cells right or down. You can also choose to insert an entire row or column. If you press this shortcut with one or more rows or columns selected, Excel inserts the same number of rows or columns without displaying the Insert dialog box.

Working with Formulas

If you construct your own worksheets, you'll probably spend a fair amount of time working with formulas. If you type those formulas, you'll be glad to know that Excel provides plenty of keyboard shortcuts for working with formulas.

Shortcuts for Working with Formulas

Start creating a formula

You can also start creating a formula by typing + or -, but = is the standard way of starting a formula.

Return

Enter the formula in the cell

After you've completed the formula, press Return to enter it in the cell. Pressing Return is the equivalent of clicking the Enter button, and usually much more convenient.

Control - Shift - Return

Enter the formula as an array formula

An *array formula* works on a range of cells (an *array*) to perform multiple calculations that generate either a single result or multiple results. Excel displays braces ({}) around an array formula to differentiate it from a regular formula.

Control - `

Toggle between displaying formula results and formulas

By default, Excel displays formula results in cells. You can display the formulas themselves by pressing this shortcut or by selecting the Formulas check box on the View tab of the Options dialog box (Tools | Options). Note that the key is the single quote mark (`), not the apostrophe.

Shift - F3

Display the Paste Function dialog box

When working in a formula, press this shortcut to display the Paste Function dialog box so that you can paste a function in a formula.

Control - A

Display the Function Arguments dialog box

When constructing a formula, move the insertion point to just after a function name, and then press this shortcut to display the Function Arguments dialog box, which walks you through supplying the correct arguments for the function.

Control -Shift -A

Enter the argument names in the Formula bar

When constructing a formula, move the insertion point to just after a function name, and then press this shortcut to enter the argument names as placeholders in the Formula bar:

Excel then moves the highlight along as you replace each placeholder in turn with valid data or a valid reference.

⌘ -Shift -T

Insert an AutoSum formula in the active cell

 Pressing this shortcut is the equivalent of clicking the AutoSum button on the Standard toolbar.

Control -Shift -"

Copy the value of the cell above the active cell

This shortcut makes Excel copy the value from the cell above the active cell into the active cell.

Control -'

Copy the formula from the cell above the active cell

This shortcut makes Excel copy the formula from the cell above the active cell into the active cell.

Recalculating Worksheets and Workbooks

Excel normally recalculates all cells in a workbook automatically when the value in any cell changes. But if you work with complex workbooks, you may need to turn off automatic recalculation (on the Calculation tab of the Options dialog box) to prevent lengthy recalculation from slowing down your work. You can then force recalculation manually when needed.

Shortcuts for Recalculating Worksheets and Workbooks

⌘-=

Recalculate all the worksheets in all the open workbooks

This command recalculates all the cells that have changed and the cells they affect. If the workbooks are highly complex, recalculation may take a long time.

Shift-F9

Recalculate the active worksheet only

If your changes are limited to the active worksheet, use this shortcut to restrict recalculation to that worksheet.

>> *Note: If you're using Jaguar, you can use Shift-F9 to recalculate the active worksheet. Panther uses F9 for Exposé's Show All Windows feature, and pressing Shift with F9 simply slows down the animation. But if you reassign the All Windows keyboard shortcut on the Exposé sheet of System Preferences (⌘ | System Preferences), you can use this shortcut in Excel on Panther too.*

Formatting Cells

Excel provides a wide range of formatting for both the contents of cells and their appearance so that the cells show exactly the data you want, in the right format, and with the appropriate emphasis. You can apply most cell formatting using the keyboard.

Shortcuts for Formatting Cells

⌘-Shift-L

Display the Style dialog box

⌘-1

Display the Format Cells dialog box

This shortcut works only with the 1 key in the key row, not the 1 key on the keypad.

Control-Shift-~
  Apply the General format

Control-Shift-$
  Apply the two-decimal-place Currency format

Control-Shift-%
  Apply the Percentage format (no decimal places)

Control-Shift-^
  Apply the Exponential format with two decimal places

Control-Shift-#
  Apply the DD-MMM-YY date format

Control-Shift-@
  Apply the HH:MM AM/PM time format

Control-Shift-!
  Apply the two-decimal-place number format with the thousands separator

⌘-Shift--
  Toggle strikethrough

⌘-Shift-W
  Toggle a shadow on text

⌘-Shift-D
  Toggle an outline on text

Shortcuts for Applying Borders

Excel includes shortcuts for applying and removing an outline border by using the keyboard.

⌘-Option-0
  Apply an outline border on the selection

This shortcut uses the zero rather than the letter O.

⌘-Option-‐

Remove the outline border from the selection

⌘-Option-→

Toggle an outline border on the right border of the selection

⌘-Option-←

Toggle an outline border on the left border of the selection

⌘-Option-↑

Toggle an outline border on the top border of the selection

⌘-Option-↓

Toggle an outline border on the bottom border of the selection

Control-Shift-_

Remove the outline border

Working in Outlines

Excel's outlining features enable you to collapse large worksheets so that only the parts you need to see appear on screen. For most outlining actions, you must use the mouse, but you can toggle the display of outline symbols from the keyboard.

Shortcuts for Working in Outlines

Control-8

Toggle the display of outline symbols

You can hide outline symbols to reclaim the space that they take up on screen. Redisplay the symbols when you need to work with them again.

When working in outlines, you'll often need to hide and unhide rows and columns, as discussed next.

Hiding and Unhiding Rows and Columns

Excel provides shortcuts for quickly hiding and unhiding rows and columns from the keyboard. To hide rows or columns, select them before pressing the shortcut. To unhide rows or columns, select cells in the rows or columns around them, and then press the shortcut.

Shortcuts for Hiding and Unhiding Rows and Columns

Control-9
  Hide all selected rows

Control-0
  Hide all selected columns

Control-Shift-((
  Unhide hidden rows in the selection

Control-Shift-()
  Unhide hidden columns in the selection

Creating and Navigating in Charts

Charts are a quintessentially graphical item, but Excel also provides a couple of keyboard shortcuts worth knowing. You can access a chart sheet just as you would any other worksheet, by pressing Control-PageDown (to move to the next worksheet) or Control-PageUp (to move to the previous worksheet) until the chart sheet is selected.

» Note: *If you're using Jaguar, you can use F11 to create a new default chart from the selected data. Panther uses F11 for Exposé's Show The Desktop feature. But if you reassign the Desktop keyboard shortcut on the Exposé sheet of System Preferences (| System Preferences), you can use this shortcut in Excel on Panther too.*

Shortcuts for Creating and Navigating in Charts

F11

Create a chart from the selected range

This shortcut creates a chart using the default chart type. If you often create charts of the same type, you can customize the default chart setting. To do so, follow these steps:

1. Right-click a chart and choose Chart Type from the shortcut menu to display the Chart Type dialog box. Alternatively, select the chart and choose Chart | Chart Type.

2. Select the chart type on the Standard Types tab or the Custom Types tab.

Excel

3. Click the Set As Default Chart button. Excel displays a confirmation dialog box.

4. Click the Yes button.

5. Click the OK button to close the Chart Type dialog box.

⟨←⟩, ⟨→⟩, ⟨↑⟩, ⟨↓⟩

Select the next chart component in the direction of the arrow

For example, press ⟨→⟩ to select the next item to the right of the currently selected item.

Working in PivotTables

Like charts, PivotTables are largely graphical items for which the mouse tends to be much more convenient than the keyboard. Nevertheless, if you work extensively with PivotTables, you may benefit from knowing the keyboard shortcuts that Excel offers for working with them.

Shortcuts for Working in PivotTables

⟨Control⟩-⟨Shift⟩-⟨*⟩

Select the entire PivotTable

Select the entire PivotTable when you want to take an action with it—for example, to apply formatting to the whole PivotTable.

⟨←⟩, ⟨→⟩, ⟨↑⟩, ⟨↓⟩

Navigate from item to item in the PivotTable

⟨Option⟩-⟨↓⟩

Display the selected drop-down list

You can navigate the drop-down list by pressing ⟨↓⟩ to move down, ⟨↑⟩ to move up, ⟨End⟩ to select the last visible item, and ⟨Home⟩ to select the first visible item.

⟨Spacebar⟩

Select, clear, or double-check a check box

Double-checking a check box selects the check boxes for the item's subitems as well.

Working in Data Forms

To help you enter data in a database more easily, Excel offers *data forms*—custom dialog boxes that Excel creates using the fields that make up the database. Excel provides keyboard shortcuts for navigating within and among data forms.

Shortcuts for Working in Data Forms

Control - Page Down
Insert a new, blank record in the database

Return
Move to the next record, first field

Shift - Return
Move to the previous record, first field

↓
Move to the next record, same field
Excel selects the same field in the next record that was active in the current record.

↑
Move to the previous record, same field
Excel selects the same field in the previous record that was active in the current record.

Page Down
Move ten records forward, same field

Page Up
Move ten records backward, same field

Working in Print Preview

Print Preview is easy to navigate with the mouse, but you can also navigate effectively with the keyboard if you know which keys to press.

Keyboard Shortcuts for Working in Print Preview

Control - ↑ , Control - ←
Display to the first page of the print area
This shortcut works only when Print Preview is zoomed out.

 ,

Display the last page of the print area

This shortcut works only when Print Preview is zoomed out.

[Page Up]

Display the previous page

This shortcut works only when Print Preview is zoomed out.

[Page Down]

Display the next page

This shortcut works only when Print Preview is zoomed out.

Move around the page

This shortcut works only when Print Preview is zoomed in.

Customizing Excel to Add Your Shortcuts

As you've seen so far in this chapter, Excel comes with an impressive number of keyboard shortcuts already built in. But if you use Excel extensively, you'll probably benefit from adding keyboard shortcuts of your own or customizing the built-in keyboard shortcuts. Excel lets you do this with great ease.

Creating Keyboard Shortcuts

To create a new keyboard shortcut in Excel, follow these steps:

1. Choose Tools | Customize to display the Customize dialog box.

2. Click the Keyboard button on either of the sheets to display the Customize Keyboard dialog box. To enable you to see all the components of the Customize Keyboard dialog box, Figure 5-1 shows the dialog box with an assignment under way.

3. In the Categories list box, select the category of item for which you want to create or change the keyboard shortcut. The list box to the right of the Categories list box changes its name to match the category you select.

   - The All Commands category lists the full list of Excel commands. Because there are so many commands, this list is awkward to use, so you'll probably want to use it only when you can't remember which menu a command is associated with.

   - Each of the eight menu categories (File, Edit, View, Insert, Format, Tools, Data, and Window and Help) lists the commands associated with that menu. The more often used commands appear on the menus, while the less used commands don't appear. For example, the Print command appears on the File menu, while the Toggle Read Only command doesn't appear.

- The Drawing category lists the commands associated with the Drawing toolbar.

- The AutoShapes category lists the commands associated with the AutoShapes available on the Drawing toolbar.

- The Charting category lists the commands associated with the Chart menu and the Chart toolbar.

- The Forms category lists the commands associated with working in forms.

- The Web category lists the commands associated with the Web toolbar and web-related actions.

4. In the right list box, select the command for which you want to create or change a keyboard shortcut. Excel displays any existing keyboard shortcut for the command in the Current Keys list box.

5. Press ⌘-Ⓝ or click in the Press New Shortcut Key text box to put the focus there.

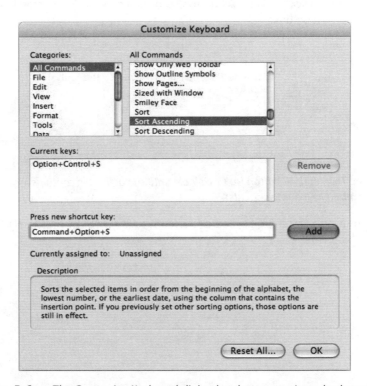

Figure 5-1   *The Customize Keyboard dialog box lets you assign a keyboard shortcut to almost any command.*

6. Press the keyboard shortcut you want to assign. If this shortcut is currently assigned to another command, Excel displays the Currently Assigned To line listing the command, so that you'll know which existing shortcut you're about to overwrite. Choose a different keyboard shortcut if necessary.

7. Click the Assign button to assign the keyboard shortcut to the command.

8. Assign further keyboard shortcuts as necessary.

9. Click the Close button to close the Customize Keyboard dialog box.

10. Click the Close button to close the Customize dialog box.

After adding keyboard shortcuts, save the file by pressing ⌘-Ⓢ or Ⓢʰⁱᶠᵗ-F12.

Removing and Resetting Keyboard Shortcuts

To remove a keyboard shortcut, display the Customize Keyboard dialog box, specify which document or template you want to affect, and select the command so that Excel displays the current keyboard shortcut. Select the shortcut in the Current Keys list box, and then click the Remove button.

To reset all keyboard shortcuts in the specified document or template to their default settings, click the Reset All button, and then click the Yes button in the confirmation dialog box:

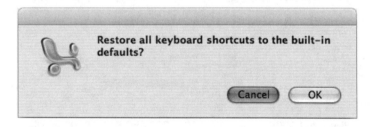

>> **Note:** *The Reset All button isn't available until the active file contains customized keyboard shortcuts.*

After removing or resetting keyboard shortcuts, save the file by pressing ⌘-Ⓢ or Ⓢʰⁱᶠᵗ-F12.

6

PowerPoint Keyboard Shortcuts

Although PowerPoint is a relatively visual application, you can take many actions in it by using the keyboard. PowerPoint supports keyboard shortcuts for creating the text of presentations, formatting it, and spell-checking it; for running presentations; and for working your way through web-based presentations. As you might expect, PowerPoint lacks shortcuts for its most graphical features, such as creating and formatting AutoShapes. For working with graphical objects, you're much better off using the mouse.

Notes on the Standard Shortcuts

PowerPoint supports the standard Office keyboard shortcuts discussed in "Shared Keyboard Shortcuts" in Chapter 3. The following exceptions are worth noting.

Shortcuts for Creating a New Presentation

⌘-Shift-P

Display the Project Gallery

From the Project Gallery, you can create a new document in any of the Office applications, using any of the available templates.

⌘-N

Create a new presentation

Pressing ⌘-N creates a new presentation using the default template and displays the New Slide dialog box (Figure 6-1) to allow you to select which layout to use for the first slide.

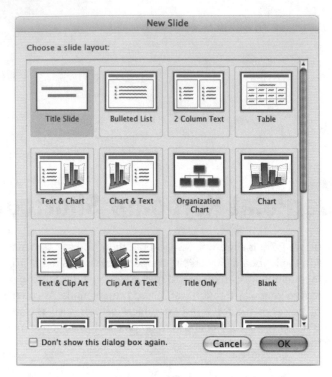

Figure 6-1 In the New Slide dialog box, choose the layout to use for the first slide in the new presentation.

Shortcuts for Moving in Text

Option - Return

Select the next title placeholder or body text placeholder, or insert a new slide

Use this shortcut to move from one placeholder to another with the keyboard. When the currently selected placeholder is the last placeholder on a slide, pressing this shortcut inserts a new slide in the presentation after the active slide.

⌘ - End

Move the insertion point to the end of a text box

⌘ - Home

Move the insertion point to the beginning of a text box

Creating a Presentation

When creating a presentation, you can use the keyboard shortcuts that PowerPoint offers for inserting new slides and duplicating existing slides, toggling Print Preview, searching for the next instance of the current search term, and finding the next spelling error.

Shortcuts for Creating a Presentation and Its Contents

[Control]-[M]

Insert a new slide

This shortcut is the equivalent of choosing Insert | New Slide.

[⌘]-[D]

Duplicate the selected slide

Duplicate a slide when you need to base another slide on it. This shortcut works in Outline view and Slide Sorter view, and in the Outline pane in Normal view.

[⌘]-[Shift]-[D]

Duplicate the selected slide

This shortcut works in Notes Page view and in the Slide pane and the Notes pane in Normal view.

[⌘]-[Shift]-[H]

Display the Replace dialog box

[Option]-[Shift]-[F7]

Display the dictionary

[⌘]-[Option]-[L]

Start a spelling check

You can use this shortcut as well as [F7] to start a spelling check.

[⌘]-[G]

Toggle the display of guidelines

PowerPoint

The guidelines (which you can also toggle by choosing View | Guides) appear as dotted horizontal and vertical lines across the middle of the slide. Use the guidelines to help you position objects.

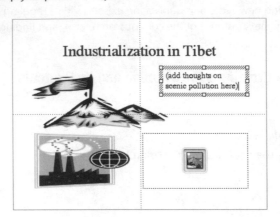

Control-Shift-Z

Switch to Normal view

You can use this keyboard shortcut and the next two shortcuts to change views instead of using the View menu or the View buttons:

Normal View   Slide View   Slide Show

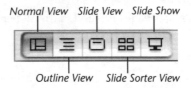

Outline View   Slide Sorter View

Control-Shift-V

Switch to Slide Sorter view

Control-Shift-T

Switch to Notes view

Control-Shift-X

Expand the Outline pane

Control-Shift-C

Expand the Slide pane

> **Tip:** Shift-*click the Outline View button or the Slide Sorter View button to access Handout Master view.* Shift-*click the Slide View button to access Slide Master view.* Shift-*click the Slide Show button to display the Set Up Show dialog box.*

Working on the Outline for a Presentation

Because the outline for a presentation consists of text, you can save time when working on an outline by using the keyboard shortcuts that PowerPoint provides. You can use these shortcuts either when the focus is in the Outline pane or when the focus is in a paragraph on a slide.

Shortcuts for Working on Outlines

(Option)-(Shift)-(←)

Promote the active paragraph to the next level

For example, click in a heading level 2 paragraph and press this shortcut to promote the paragraph to heading level 1.

(Option)-(Shift)-(→)

Demote the active paragraph to the next level

(Option)-(Shift)-(↑)

Move the selected paragraphs up by one displayed item

This shortcut and the next move the selection by one displayed item at a time. If a slide is collapsed, it counts as one item; if it is expanded, it counts as multiple items. Either expand or collapse the outline before pressing this shortcut, or use the shortcut multiple times.

(Option)-(Shift)-(↓)

Move the selected paragraphs down by one displayed item

(Option)-(Shift)-(1) on the numeric keypad

Show heading level 1

This shortcut collapses the outline to display only heading level 1 paragraphs.

(Option)-(Shift)-(+) on the numeric keypad

Expand the headings and text below the selected heading

Select a heading and press this shortcut to expand all the headings and text below it.

(Option)-(Shift)-(-) on the numeric keypad

Collapse the headings and text below the selected heading

Select a heading and press this shortcut to collapse all the headings and text below it.

PowerPoint

You can use the following shortcuts to promote and demote paragraphs when working in the Outline pane. You can also use these shortcuts when working on a slide provided that the insertion point is before the first letter in the line.

Demote the active paragraph to the next level

Shift - Tab

Promote the active paragraph to the next level

Selecting Objects

To select an object using the keyboard, you move the focus by pressing Tab or Shift - Tab. Before these keys will move the focus, you must press Esc if the insertion point is currently positioned in text. Pressing Esc moves the focus from the text to the object that contains it.

Shortcuts for Selecting Objects

Cycle forward through the objects on the slide

PowerPoint displays selection handles around the object that currently has the focus.

The Pleasure of the Sierra Madre

Shift - Tab

Cycle backward through the objects on the slide

After selecting an object, you can move it by pressing ←, →, ↑, and ↓. For example, press ↓ to move the object downward from its current position.

⌘ - A

Select all objects or all text

In Slide view or Slide Sorter view, press ⌘-A to select all objects. In Outline view, press ⌘-A to select all text.

Applying Formatting

To make any presentation look not only good but also powerful, convincing, or persuasive, you'll need to format its text and objects carefully. You can do much (sometimes all) of your formatting work from the keyboard.

Shortcuts for Applying Formatting

⌘-Shift-F

Select the Font drop-down list on the Formatting toolbar

⌘-Shift->

Increase the font size in jumps

⌘-Shift-<

Decrease the font size in jumps

⌘-T

Display the Font dialog box

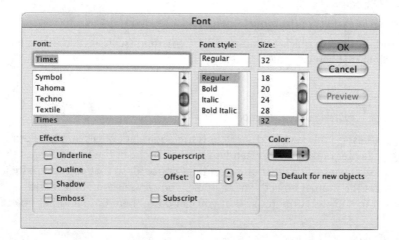

Shift-F3

Cycle the case of the selection

This shortcut cycles the case among lowercase, title case (the first letter of each word is capitalized), and uppercase (all letters are capitalized). This shortcut is an alternative to the Format | Change Case command, but that command also offers a Sentence Case option (the first letter of each sentence is capitalized) and a tOGGLE cASE command (PowerPoint inverts the capitalization of each letter).

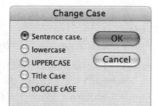

⌘-=

Toggle subscript

Subscript decreases the font size of the selected text and lowers it below the baseline of the other characters.

》 Note: *The Superscript and Subscript check boxes and Offset text box in the Effects group box in the Font dialog box (⌘-T) give you more precise control over subscripts and superscripts.*

⌘-Shift-+

Toggle superscript

Superscript decreases the font size of the selected text and raises it above the baseline of the other characters.

Control-Spacebar

Reset the formatting of the current paragraph or selection

Use this shortcut to quickly remove direct formatting (such as bold, italic, and underline) that you've applied to text.

⌘-Shift-C

Copy the formatting of the selection

 Pressing this keyboard shortcut is the equivalent of clicking the Format Painter button on the Standard toolbar: it copies the formatting of the selected text or other object to the Clipboard, so that you can paste it to other text (or another object). For example, you can select an object and use this shortcut to copy its attributes so that you can paste them onto another object.

⌘-Shift-V

Apply the copied formatting to the selection

After copying formatting using Control-Shift-C (or by clicking the Format Painter button), apply the formatting to its destination by using this shortcut or by clicking the Format Painter button.

⌘-J

Apply justified alignment to the paragraph

Applying justified alignment to (or "justifying") a paragraph aligns the left end of its lines with the left margin and the right end of its lines with the right margin. The last line isn't aligned with the right margin unless it happens to reach the margin anyway.

Running a Slide Show

Most presenters stick with the mouse when giving their presentations, which works fine for advancing the presentation but leaves them stuck fumbling with the context menu and its submenus when they need to execute any other command. If you put in the modicum of effort required to learn the keyboard shortcuts that PowerPoint provides for running a slide show, you can control the presentation faster and more easily, which gives a more professional appearance to your presentation.

Shortcuts for Running a Slide Show

Control - Shift - S

Start a slide show from the first slide

Press this shortcut instead of choosing Slide Show | View Show.

Control - Shift - B

Start a slide show from the current slide

Navigate to the slide from which you want to start the slide show, and then press this shortcut. Alternatively, click the Slide Show button.

Esc, ⌘, ., -

End the slide show

Esc is the easiest shortcut for ending a presentation.

N, Return, Spacebar, ↓, →, Page Down

Display the next animation or the next slide

Press any of these keys to trigger the next animation (if there is one) or display the next slide (if there is no further animation).

P, Delete, ↑, ←, Page Up

Display the previous animation or the previous slide

Press any of these keys to trigger the previous animation (if there is one) or display the previous slide (if there is no previous animation).

Number, then Return

Display the slide identified by the number

For example, press 5, then Return to display slide 5 in the presentation.

[B], [.]

Toggle a black screen

Press [B] or [.] to display a black screen in place of the current slide. Press [B] or [.] again to display the slide again.

[W], [,]

Toggle a white screen

Press [W] or [,] to display a white screen in place of the current slide. Press [W] or [,] again to display the slide again.

[S], [+]

Stop or restart an automatic slide show

If you've set a slide show to run automatically, press [S] or [+] to stop or restart it.

[⌘]-[P]

Redisplay the hidden pointer, or change the pointer to a pen

If the pointer is hidden, press [⌘]-[P] to restore it. If the pointer is displayed, press [⌘]-[P] to change the pointer to a pen. (You can use the pen to make annotations on the screen.)

[E]

Erase all on-screen annotations

Use this shortcut to erase any annotations you've made using the pen.

[H]

Display the next hidden slide

Use hidden slides to keep extra information up your sleeve.

[T]

Apply new timings while rehearsing

[O]

Use your original timings while rehearsing

[M]

Toggle to using the mouse to advance while rehearsing

, ⟨=⟩

Toggle hiding on the pointer

⟨Control⟩-⟨H⟩

Hide the pointer and button temporarily

⟨Control⟩-⟨U⟩

Hide the pointer after ten seconds, or redisplay the pointer

If the mouse pointer is displayed, press ⟨Control⟩-⟨U⟩ to hide the pointer ten seconds after you press the keys. When the mouse pointer is hidden, press ⟨Control⟩-⟨U⟩ to redisplay it immediately.

⟨Control⟩-click

Display the shortcut menu

After displaying the shortcut menu, you can use the arrow keys on the keyboard to navigate to the choice you want to make, and then press ⟨Return⟩.

Browsing Hyperlinks and Web Presentations

If a slide show contains hyperlinks, you can browse them by using the keyboard instead of the mouse. Similarly, you can use the keyboard to browse a web presentation in Internet Explorer 4 or a later version.

Shortcuts for Browsing the Hyperlinks in a Slide Show

⟨Tab⟩

Select the next hyperlink

⟨Shift⟩-⟨Tab⟩

Select the previous hyperlink

⟨Return⟩

Click the selected hyperlink

Navigate to the hyperlink you want to follow, and then press ⟨Return⟩ to click it.

⟨Shift⟩-⟨Return⟩

Trigger the mouse-over action for the hyperlink

The *mouse-over action* is the action that occurs when you move the mouse pointer over the hyperlink.

Shortcuts for Browsing a Web Presentation

Use the following keyboard shortcuts to browse a web presentation in Internet Explorer 4 or a later version.

Tab

Move to the next hyperlink, to the Address bar, or to the Links bar

Press Tab to navigate to the next element in the presentation.

Shift-Tab

Move to the previous hyperlink, to the Address bar, or to the Links bar

Press Shift-Tab to navigate to the previous element in the presentation.

Spacebar

Display the next slide

Delete

Display the previous slide

7

Entourage Keyboard Shortcuts

After Word, Entourage is perhaps the most text-based of the Office applications, so it's no surprise that Entourage offers plenty of keyboard shortcuts. This chapter starts by discussing Entourage's exceptions from Office's standard shortcuts, then moves along to explain the shortcuts that work for all areas of Entourage before examining the shortcuts for the different areas: the Mail list (which has a large number of keyboard shortcuts), the Calendar, the Address Book, the Notes list, and the Tasks list.

Notes on the Standard Shortcuts

Entourage supports most of the standard Office keyboard shortcuts discussed in "Shared Keyboard Shortcuts" in Chapter 3. The following exceptions are worth noting.

Shortcuts for Creating New Items

In Entourage, you can create various types of items (such as messages, tasks, notes, and contacts), so Entourage offers various keyboard shortcuts for creating items rather than just the standard ⌘-N keyboard shortcut. You'll learn about these shortcuts later in this chapter.

⌘-Shift-P

Display the Project Gallery

From the Project Gallery, you can create a new document in any of the Office applications, using any of the available templates. But for creating an Entourage item, it's usually quicker to use a keyboard shortcut directly from Entourage.

Shortcuts for Opening and Deleting Items

Because Entourage doesn't work with files in the same way as the other Office applications, it uses a different method of opening items.

⌘-O

Open the selected folder or item in a new window

Select a folder in the Folders list, or an item in another list, and then press ⌘-O to open it.

⌘-Delete

Delete the selected item

Shortcuts for Printing Items

Besides supporting the standard ⌘-P shortcut for displaying the Print dialog box, Entourage offers a shortcut for printing without displaying the Print dialog box.

⌘-Option-P

Print the item using default settings

Press this shortcut to print one copy of the selected item using default print settings and without displaying the Print dialog box.

Shortcuts for Setting Preferences

Unlike most Mac OS X applications, Entourage doesn't use the ⌘-, shortcut for displaying the Preferences dialog box. (Instead, Entourage uses ⌘-, to assign the selected item to a category.) Entourage offers different keyboard shortcuts for displaying the General Preferences dialog box and the Mail & News Preferences dialog box.

⌘-;

Display the General Preferences dialog box

The General Preferences dialog box contains tabs for General preferences, Address Book preferences, Calendar preferences, Fonts preferences, Spelling preferences, and Notification preferences.

⌘-Shift-;

Display the Mail & News Preferences dialog box

The Mail & News Preferences dialog box contains tabs for Read preferences, Compose preferences, Reply & Forward preferences, View preferences, and Proxies preferences.

Shortcuts for Pasting Text

Entourage supports the standard Mac OS X keyboard shortcuts for Cut (⌘-Ⓧ), Copy (⌘-Ⓒ), and Paste (⌘-Ⓥ). But Entourage also offers two custom shortcuts for pasting text.

⌘-Shift-Ⓥ

Paste the text from the Clipboard as a quotation

⌘-Option-Ⓥ

Paste the text from the Clipboard as plain text

Pasting text as plain text removes any formatting from the text.

Shortcuts for Switching Identity

Instead of quitting Entourage (press ⌘-Ⓠ as usual), you can switch identity within Entourage by using the following shortcut.

⌘-Option-Ⓠ

Switch to a different identity

When you press ⌘-Option-Ⓠ (or choose Entourage | Switch Identity), Entourage displays the dialog box shown on the left here to ensure that you haven't issued the command by accident. Click the Switch button to proceed. (If you want to be able to switch identity in the future without seeing this confirmation dialog box, select the Don't Show This Message Again check box.) Entourage then closes all connections and windows, and displays the Entourage dialog box shown on the right here. Select the identity to use, and then click the OK button.

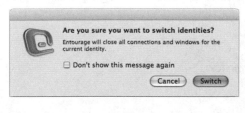
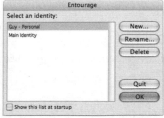

Shortcuts for Working with Windows

Entourage includes powerful shortcuts for quickly displaying the element you want to work with, either in the same window or in a new window, and for switching quickly among the available views.

⌘-Option-W

Close the active window and all open items

This shortcut is like the standard ⌘-W shortcut (for closing the active window) on steroids.

⌘-Option-Shift-N

Open a new Entourage window

Press this shortcut to open a new Entourage window showing the active item.

⌘-~

Cycle forward through the open windows

Use this shortcut and the next shortcut to move quickly from one Entourage window to another. (To move between Entourage and other open windows, use ⌘-Tab and ⌘-Shift-Tab as usual. Alternatively, use the Exposé keystrokes.)

⌘-Shift-~

Cycle backward through the open windows

⌘-1

Display the Mail list

If you have multiple e-mail accounts in the Folders list, you can press ⌘-1 again to cycle through the accounts.

⌘-Option-1

Display the Mail list in a new window

⌘-2

Display the Address book

If your Address book contains custom views, you can press ⌘-2 again to cycle through the custom views.

⌘-Option-2

Display the Address book in a new window

⌘-3

Display the Calendar

You can press ⌘-3 again to cycle through Day view, Work Week view, Week view, and Month view.

⌘-Option-3

Display the Calendar in a new window

⌘-4

Display the Notes list

If your Notes list contains custom views, you can press ⌘-4 again to cycle through the custom views.

⌘-Option-4

Display the Notes list in a new window

⌘-5

Display the Tasks list

If your Tasks list contains custom views, you can press ⌘-5 again to cycle through the custom views.

⌘-Option-5

Display the Tasks list in a new window

⌘-6

Display the Custom Views list

Press ⌘-6 again to cycle through the custom views.

⌘-7

Display the Progress window

Use the Progress window (shown here) to see which operations Entourage is currently performing. If an operation takes too long, you can stop it by clicking the appropriate Stop button. To stop all operations, click the Stop All button.

⌘-8

Display the Link Maker window

Use the Link Maker window (shown here) to create a link between two items. Drag the first item and drop it on the Link From box, and then drag the second item and drop it on the Link To box.

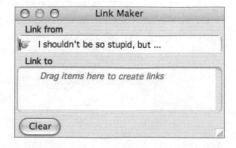

Entourage

⌘-9

Display the Error Log window

Shortcuts for Finding Text

Beyond the standard ⌘-F keyboard shortcut for displaying the Find dialog box (shown here), Entourage offers the following keyboard shortcuts for finding text.

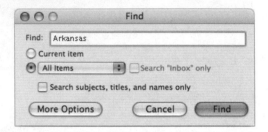

⌘-G

Find the next instance of the search text

After performing a Find operation and finding an instance of the search text, you can press this shortcut to find the next instance of the search text in the same item (for example, a message) without displaying the Find dialog box.

⌘-Shift-G

Find the next instance of the search text

⌘-.

Cancel the current search

If a search is taking too long, press ⌘-. to cancel it.

⌘-Option-F

Display the Advanced section of the Find dialog box

Use the Advanced section of the Find dialog box (shown next) to create more targeted searches. You can also display the Advanced section of the Find dialog box by clicking the More Options button in the basic section of the Find dialog box (and return to the basic section of the Find dialog box by clicking the Fewer Options button in the Advanced section).

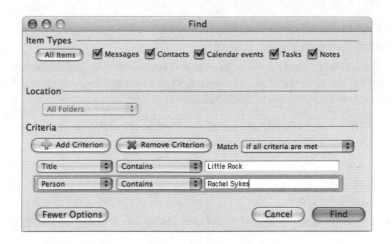

Working in All Areas of Entourage

Apart from the shortcuts that work only in specific areas of its functionality (for example, in the Mail list), Entourage offers a number of shortcuts that work in all areas.

Shortcuts for Working in All Areas of Entourage

⌘-Option-Shift-N

Display the current list in a new window

For example, press ⌘-Option-Shift-N from the Mail list to display the Mail list in a new window.

⌘-N

Create a new item

Press this shortcut to create a new item in the current list. For example, press ⌘-N in the Mail list to create a new message, press ⌘-N in the Address Book to create a new contact, or press ⌘-N in Calendar to create a new appointment.

⌘-A

Select all the items in the list

For this shortcut to work, you must make the appropriate list the active pane first. For example, to select all the messages in the Mail list, make the Mail list the active pane, and then press ⌘-A.

Entourage

⌘-Shift-A

Deselect all the selected items in the list

For this shortcut to work, you must make the appropriate list the active pane first. For example, to select all the contacts in the Address Book, make the Address Book the active pane, and then press ⌘-Shift-A.

» Note: *If you've previously selected all the items in the list you're working in, the appropriate list should already be the active pane.*

⌘-O

Open the selected item

For example, to open a note, select it in the Notes list, and then press ⌘-O.

⌘-D

Duplicate the selected item

⌘-Delete

Delete the selected item

When you press this shortcut for any item except a message, Entourage displays a confirmation dialog box such as the one shown here. Press D or click the Delete button to delete the item.

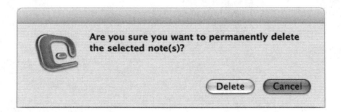

⌘-[

Close the open contact and display the previous contact

Press this shortcut when you need to close the window containing a contact and display a window containing the previous contact.

⌘-]

Close the open item and display the next item

Press this shortcut when you need to close the window containing an item and display a window containing the next item.

⌘-,

Display the Assign Categories dialog box

In the Assign Categories dialog box, select the check boxes for the categories you want to assign to the item, and then click the OK button.

⌘-S

Make the selected category the primary category for the item

When you've assigned multiple categories to an item, you can change the primary category assigned to the item by displaying the Assign Categories dialog box (press ⌘-,), selecting the category you want to make primary, pressing this shortcut or clicking the Set Primary button, and then pressing Return or clicking the OK button.

Working in the Mail List

If your job is halfway normal, you'll spend much of your time in Entourage working with messages: writing new messages and replies, forwarding messages to your more accommodating colleagues, filing messages in the hopes of reaching the bottom of your Inbox, and deleting virtual reams of spam. You can do all this from the keyboard.

Shortcuts for Working in the Mail List

⌘-L

Refresh the Mail list

This shortcut works only for IMAP accounts, Hotmail accounts, and online POP accounts. (POP is the abbreviation for Post Office Protocol, the most widely used protocol for transferring mail. IMAP is the abbreviation for Internet Mail Access Protocol, a more sophisticated protocol for transferring mail.)

⌘-Option-N

Create a new message from anywhere in Entourage

Because this keyboard shortcut works from any area of Entourage, you might choose to use it as your standard keystroke for creating a new message, even when you're working in the Mail list.

⌘-Shift-N

Create a new folder in the current folder

Select the appropriate folder in the Folders list before pressing this shortcut.

Entourage

⌘-Delete

Delete the selected message

When you press this shortcut, Entourage moves the message to your Deleted Items folder without confirmation. You can recover the message from your Deleted Items folder until you empty that folder.

⌘-\

Toggle the display of the Preview pane

⌘-Shift-O

Toggle the display of unread messages only

Press this shortcut to display only unread messages in the selected folder (in other words, to make Entourage hide the messages you've read). Press this shortcut again to restore the display of read messages.

⌘-Option-O

Toggle the display of flagged messages only

Press this shortcut to display only flagged messages in the selected folder (in other words, to make Entourage hide all messages that don't have flags set on them). Press this shortcut again to restore the display of unflagged messages.

⌘-T

Mark the selected messages as read

⌘-Shift-T

Mark the selected messages as unread

⌘-Option-T

Mark all the messages in the selected folder as read

Shortcuts for Reading Messages

⌘-O

Open the selected message in a new window

⌘-'

Flag the selected message

⌘-Shift-'

Flag the selected message for follow-up

Delete

Delete the selected message

⌘-=

Add the sender of the selected message to your Address Book

⌘-Shift-M

Display the Move dialog box

In the Move dialog box, select the folder to which you want to move the selected message, and then press Return or click the Move button.

⌘-Shift--

Reduce the text size in the open message or the Preview pane

⌘-Shift-=

Increase the text size in the open message or the Preview pane

⌘-Shift-H

Toggle the display of Internet headers

This shortcut works only in a message window, not in the Preview pane. Internet headers can help you see which Internet host sent a message and how it traveled, which can be helpful for diagnostic purposes and for dealing with spam. Under normal circumstances, you'll seldom need to display Internet headers.

Control-[

Display the previous unread message

This shortcut is a useful addition to the standard ⌘-[shortcut, which displays the previous message whether it's read or unread.

Control-]

Display the next unread message

This shortcut is a useful addition to the standard ⌘-] shortcut, which displays the next message whether it's read or unread.

Entourage

⌘ - Option - [

Delete the current message and display the previous message

When you press this shortcut, Entourage displays the previous message whether it's read or unread.

⌘ - Option -]

Delete the current message and display the next message

When you press this shortcut, Entourage displays the next message whether it's read or unread.

Spacebar

Display the next screen or the next unread message

Press Spacebar to display the next screen of text in the current message. When you've reached the end of the message, you can press Spacebar to display the next unread message.

≫ Tip: *Press* Spacebar *and hold it down to scroll slowly through the current message.*

Shift - Spacebar

Display the previous screen

Press this shortcut to display the previous screen of text in the current message.

Option - Spacebar

Delete the message and display the next unread message

When you are at the end of a message, press this shortcut to delete the message and display the next unread message. Pressing this shortcut when not at the end of a message causes Entourage to display the next screen of text in the message, just as pressing Spacebar alone does. But unless you usually want to delete messages after reading them, it's better to use Spacebar for scrolling messages to the end and use this keyboard shortcut only when you want to delete the message and move on to the next unread message.

Control - Option - [

Delete the current message and display the previous unread message

Control - Option -]

Delete the current message and display the next unread message

Option - Delete

Delete the current message

If the message is open in a message window, Entourage closes that window.

Shortcuts for Reading Threaded Messages

Entourage provides a double-handful of keyboard shortcuts for reading *threaded messages* (messages that are related to each other).

⌘ - Shift - [

Display the last message in the previous thread

⌘ - Shift -]

Display the first message in the next thread

⌘ - Option - Shift - [

Delete the current message and display the last message in the previous thread

⌘ - Option - Shift -]

Delete the current message and display the first message in the next thread

Control - Shift - [

Display the last unread message in the previous thread that includes an unread message

Press this shortcut to move to the previous thread that contains one or more unread messages, and to display the last unread message in it.

Control - Shift -]

Display the first unread message in the next thread that includes an unread message

Press this shortcut to move to the next thread that contains one or more unread messages, and to display the first unread message in it.

Control - Option - Shift - [

Delete the current message and display the last unread message in the previous thread that includes an unread message

Control - Option - Shift -]

Delete the current message and display the first unread message in the next thread that includes an unread message

⌘-Option-Delete

Delete all messages in the current thread

Shortcuts for Creating and Sending Messages

⌘-S

Save the current message as a draft in the Drafts folder

By saving a message in the Drafts folder, you can keep it so that you can work on it later.

⌘-E

Display the Choose Attachment dialog box

In the Choose Attachment dialog box, select the file you want to attach, and then press Return or click the Open button.

⌘-Return

Send the current message

When you press this shortcut, Entourage sends the message immediately.

⌘-Shift-Return

Move the current message to the Outbox

After you move a message to the Outbox, Entourage stores it there and sends it the next time you connect to the mail server.

⌘-K

Send and receive all messages

⌘-Shift-K

Send all messages

Press this shortcut to send all messages in your Outbox without checking for incoming mail.

⌘-Option-L

Check the spelling in the current message

⌘-Shift-C

Check the names of recipients in the current message

[Option]-[Shift]-[F7]

Display the Dictionary window

Shortcuts for Replying to Messages

[⌘]-[R]

Reply to the sender of the message

This shortcut is handy for working quickly, but be careful not to use it inadvertently when reading a message from a mailing list, because it sends the reply to the entire mailing list. (Often, you'll want to reply to the person who posted the message to the list, not to the entire list.)

[⌘]-[Shift]-[R]

Reply to all recipients of the message

Replying to all recipients of a message sends replies to everyone on the To list and the CC list.

[⌘]-[J]

Forward the message

[⌘]-[Option]-[J]

Redirect the message

Redirecting a message is similar to forwarding it, but Entourage doesn't mark the message as being forwarded.

Working in the Calendar

Apart from the shortcuts common to all areas of Entourage, there are three keyboard shortcuts for working in the Calendar.

Shortcuts for Working in the Calendar

[⌘]-[T]

Display Today

Press this shortcut to display the calendar section (Day, Work Week, Week, or Month) that contains the current date.

[⌘]-[[]

Display the previous item

Pressing this standard shortcut displays the previous one of the items you're working with. For example, if you're using Week view, pressing ⌘-[displays the previous week. If you're using Month view, pressing ⌘-[displays the previous month.

Display the next item

Pressing this standard shortcut displays the next one of the items you're working with. For example, if you're using Week view, pressing ⌘-] displays the next week. If you're using Month view, pressing ⌘-] displays the next month.

Working in the Address Book

Entourage offers a couple of keyboard shortcuts for working in Address Book that are worth knowing.

Shortcuts for Working in the Address Book

Toggle the display of the Preview pane

Flag the selected contact

Working in the Notes List and Tasks List

When working in the Notes list and Tasks list, you can use all the keyboard shortcuts discussed in "Shortcuts for Working in All Areas of Entourage," earlier in this chapter. For example, you can press ⌘-Option-Shift-N to open the Notes list in a new window, press ⌘-N to create a new note, and press ⌘-] to close the current open note and display the next note. Similarly, you can press ⌘-O to open the selected task, or ⌘-Delete to delete it.

Beyond the standard shortcuts, Entourage has no Notes list–specific or Tasks list–specific keyboard shortcuts.

Choosing a Better Keyboard

Every Mac comes with a keyboard and either a mouse or touchpad. Apple has shipped a variety of different keyboards with Macs, many of which have sacrificed usability for style to a greater or lesser extent. PowerBooks and iBooks have laptop-style keyboards rather than full keyboards because they have less space available, but in the main their keyboards are comfortable to use—as you'd hope, because it's difficult to replace them.

If you're currently using the keyboard that came with your Mac, you might benefit from upgrading to a better keyboard. This appendix discusses what kinds of keyboards are available and how to choose a suitable keyboard for your needs. (For help on configuring your keyboard and choosing such accessibility options as will help you, see Chapter 1.)

Considerations for Choosing a Keyboard

At the risk of generalizing horribly, keyboards fall into three categories: conventional, serious, and specialized (or strange) keyboards. The following sections discuss these categories.

But first, here are general considerations to keep in mind when choosing a new keyboard:

- You must choose the keyboard yourself, because only you can tell whether it suits you. One person's dream ergonomic keyboard is another person's carpal tunnel of horrors.

>> Tip: *Some specialist keyboard retailers let you rent keyboards (and other gear) for a while so that you can find out whether it suits you before buying it. One example is Keyalt.com (**www.keyalt.com**) in Santa Rosa, CA.*

- Try to type for several minutes on any keyboard you're considering buying so that you can get a fair idea of its strong points and weak points.

- Generally speaking, the more expensive a keyboard is, the higher its build quality should be. But if all you need is a conventional keyboard, you should be able to find a decent one without spending a lot of money. Besides, expense doesn't necessarily bear any relation to comfort. Don't scorn a bargain or clearance keyboard if it's comfortable, solid, and meets your needs.

- If you're likely to spill coffee, soda, or water on your keyboard, or shower it with crumbs, you may prefer to stick with a cheaper keyboard so that it costs less to replace. Alternatively, make sure that a keyboard "skin" (a cover through which you use the keyboard) is available for the model you plan to buy. You may also be able to find a company that makes custom skins for any keyboard you dredge up.

>> **Note:** *If you're prepared to pay extra, you can also get special sealed keyboards designed for industrial environments. Most sealed keyboards tend to cost $100 or more. Less expensive, but adequately sealed for all but the most serious abuse, are flexible keyboards such as the Virtually Indestructible Keyboard range (available from various retailers).*

- You don't need to be suffering from carpal tunnel or RSI syndrome before you start using an ergonomic keyboard, although sadly for many people this is the normal progression. If you spend several hours or more each day typing, seriously consider an ergonomic keyboard. You should also take such steps as possible to reduce the amount of typing you do—for example, by using keyboard shortcuts, macros, and features built into your software (such as AutoCorrect or glossary features).

Here are more specific criteria to ask yourself when you lay hands on the keyboard. They're largely obvious, but you'll kick yourself if you skip them.

- Is the keyboard designed for the Mac? Because Windows PCs outnumber Macs by more than nine to one, most keyboards are designed for Windows PCs and don't have Mac-specific keys. There are hardware and software workarounds for such missing keys, but you probably won't want to go there unless the keyboard is surpassing perfection in all other departments.

- Does the keyboard have all the keys you want? If you need 16 function keys, don't settle for a keyboard with 12 function keys. If you want volume controls or a power button on your keyboard, make sure it has them.

- Are the keys arranged where you need them to be? For example, if you've set your heart on a keyboard with function keys at the side, keyboards with function keys along the top probably won't interest you. More mundanely, you might prefer specific locations for modifier keys, full-sized arrow keys, or an extra-large [Return] key.

- Are the keys the right size for you? Standard key spacing is 19 mm from the middle of one key to the middle of the next key.

- Is the key travel adequate? (*Key travel* is the distance the key moves when you press it.) Key travel of 3 mm is about standard. Many laptop keyboards necessarily have less travel.

- Do you like the "feel" of the keyboard? This is almost entirely subjective: some people like keyboards with a firm feel; others prefer a soft feel; some like a firm response and audible click when a key is pressed, others a subtler response and no audible click.

- Does it have the right type of connector for your Mac? If your Mac is recent enough to run Mac OS X at a good clip, that probably means a USB connector. Any keyboard designed for recent Macs will have a USB connector as a matter of course, so the connector should be an issue only if you're planning to use an older keyboard designed for the Apple Desktop Bus (ADB) or a custom keyboard designed for a PC. Get an ADB-to-USB connector or a PS/2-to-USB connector if necessary.

- Is the keyboard the color you want? Computer beige is the most widely used color for keyboards, but many black keyboards are available too. Beyond these colors (or noncolors), your choices are limited. The next most popular "color" after beige and black is perhaps aluminum, with several aluminum keyboards available.

All of these issues are easy enough to resolve if you can try the keyboard before you buy it. If you must buy without trying, make sure you can return the keyboard if it doesn't suit you.

Any computer store large enough to carry a variety of Macs should offer some choices of keyboards as well, perhaps with some models on display for you to try before you buy. While large stores typically have some of the more widely used ergonomic keyboards, if you need a specialized model, you'll probably do better to visit a specialized computer-ergonomics store.

Why Wireless Keyboards Can Threaten Your Privacy

If you don't especially appreciate having your keyboard tethered to your Mac by a six-foot cable, you may be drawn by the attractions of wireless keyboards, which let you move the keyboard freely within a room's distance or so of your computer. But before you invest in a wireless keyboard, be clear on the problems that they can bring with them.

The main problem is that a wireless keyboard can transmit signals to other wireless receivers in the neighborhood. In one documented instance in Stavanger, Norway, the user of an HP wireless keyboard found that his computer was receiving signals transmitted from another wireless keyboard. From the contents, he learned that the other wireless keyboard was 150 meters (500 feet) and several walls removed from his computer.

Choosing a Better Keyboard

The wireless keyboard was transmitting to its own computer as well as to the remote computer.

The second, and secondary, problem is that you typically won't know if your wireless keyboard is transmitting what you type to another computer as well as to your own. Unless your keystrokes fail to show up on your computer, there's no reason for you to suspect a problem until you receive the unwelcome news from a neighbor who is receiving the keystrokes as well.

Conventional Keyboards

Conventional Mac keyboards are like those layouts you saw earlier in this chapter. Most Mac desktop keyboards contain between 101 and 115 keys, while most PowerBook and iBook keyboards have between 77 and 82 keys (some of which perform additional functions using the Fn key).

Serious Keyboards

The next category of keyboards is best classed as "serious"—keyboards that are more or less conventional in shape and layout but are designed for heavy-duty work.

If you find that conventional keyboards are too flimsy or have too light a feel, consider what enthusiasts call a *battleship board*—a heavy-duty keyboard that includes much more metal and correspondingly less plastic than lower-priced keyboards. The main difference between battleship boards and regular keyboards is that battleship boards usually use a buckling-spring switch under each key, whereas regular keyboards use switches constructed around rubber domes of one sort or another. Buckling springs give a much more solid click (both tactile and aural) than rubber domes and feel much more solid. They're also heavier in weight, heavier duty, and more expensive. Most are designed for PCs rather than for Macs and feature PS/2 connectors rather than USB connectors.

This essential difference distinguishes most battleship boards from regular keyboards, but you'll also find other serious keyboards that don't use buckling-spring switches on the keys. Some of these serious keyboards have different layouts than standard keyboards. For example, some serious keyboards have the function keys on the left side of the keyboard instead of on the top row. Some even have two sets of function keys: one on the left side, and one on the top row. Few people need such a different layout of function keys, but you'll know if you do.

IBM used to make the best battleship boards, and their technology lives on. Perhaps the best site for battleship boards of one type or another is PCKeyboard.com (**www.pckeyboard.com**). They are a division of Unicomp, which bought keyboard technology from Lexmark International, the company that used to make the keyboards for IBM (and, before being spun off as a separate company, was part of IBM).

Specialized Keyboards

The last category of keyboards is specialized keyboards. Some people prefer to call them *strange* keyboards—and some of them are indeed strange. But if your work (or play) involves a lot of typing, a specialized keyboard can save you plenty of time, effort, and grief.

Dividing specialized keyboards into categories tends to be difficult, because there are many different types of keyboards. But here's a stab at division:

- Undersized and oversized keyboards
- Keyboards with integrated pointing devices
- Split keyboards
- Split and tilted keyboards
- Superergonomic keyboards
- Handheld keyboards

If you're in the market for a specialized keyboard, you may find that the essential division is between keyboards that use a modified version of the standard keyboard layout and keyboards that use a radically different layout. Keyboards that use a modified version of a standard layout are usually easy to get started with, because you don't have to learn entirely new typing habits. Keyboards that use radically different layouts can offer greater ergonomic benefits or ease of use, but you'll have to learn to type on them, which can involve a considerable learning curve.

If you use the same keyboard for all your data entry, learning a new keyboard layout may be sensible and easy. If you need to use various computers, you'll probably be better off using a specialized keyboard that modifies the standard keyboard layout.

Superergonomic keyboards start at around a couple hundred dollars and progress to more than a thousand, making them a serious investment. But if you're starting to suffer from repetitive stress injury (RSI)—or attempting to avoid it altogether—the investment may well make sense.

Undersized and Oversized Keyboards

The first type of specialized keyboard you may want is an undersized or oversized keyboard. Generally speaking, there are two types of undersized keyboards: space-saving keyboards designed for small working surfaces, and keyboards with smaller-than-usual keys for people with small hands. If you look hard enough, you can find space-saving keyboards that use smaller-than-usual keys as well.

If your desk or other working surface is short of space, a compact keyboard may be the answer. Some compact keyboards have no numeric keypad at all, while others have an embedded numeric keypad like those many notebooks have. If space is at a premium, consider a compact keyboard that has an integrated pointing device, such as a pointing stick, a trackball, or a touchpad. Because the pointing stick is usually located among the keys rather than requiring an area of its own, keyboards with pointing sticks tend to be the most compact solution available.

As you learned earlier in this appendix, standard key spacing for a keyboard is 19 mm from the middle of one key to the middle of the next key. If you've learned to type on a keyboard with this key spacing, and your hands aren't extra small or extra large, you'll probably find it comfortable enough. But if your hands *are* extra small, you may be better off with a keyboard that has smaller-than-usual key spacing. A couple of millimeters make a considerable difference: 17 mm spacing (which you'll find on various ultraportable laptops) is manageable for most people, but 16 mm feels very cramped. At 15 mm and smaller sizes, anyone with normal-size fingertips has to type very accurately so as not to strike one or more neighboring keys by mistake. (If you've ever handled one of the Toshiba Libretto micro-notebooks, that's 15 mm keyboard spacing.)

Undersized keyboards are relatively easy to find if you search on the Web. So are oversized keyboards—at least, keyboards with hugely oversized keys, not the fractionally larger keys (say, 20 mm or 21 mm spacing) that people with large hands might find useful. A typical oversized keyboard, such as the Big Keys Keyboard (available from various sources), has keys that are one-inch square, which is four times the size of standard keys on a typical desktop keyboard. Keys this large aren't much good for touch-typing unless you have giant hands, but they're great for industrial environments (gloved fingers) and for mild disabilities (a bigger key is easier to strike without blipping another key). Large keys can also be good for children, because the letters are easier to spot; and some models come with the keys in a variety of colors.

Keyboards with Integrated Pointing Devices

As you read in the previous section, some undersized keyboards include integrated pointing devices. Some full-size keyboards have them as well. Most of these pointing devices are pointing sticks, touchpads, or miniature trackballs, but if you search, you can also find keyboards with more esoteric pointing devices.

Some of the stranger keyboard types include advanced pointing devices. For example, the TouchStream keyboards from FingerWorks (**www.fingerworks.com**) include a custom pointing device that interprets the gestures from your hands.

Split Keyboards

Standard keyboards have been blamed for causing carpal tunnel syndrome by forcing users to hold their hands (or even wrists) parallel to each other. In fact, this supposed compulsion is largely imaginary: it's actually easier to type with your hands pointing inward at a natural angle even on a regular keyboard.

Even so, many users find split keyboards more comfortable than regular keyboards. In a split keyboard layout, the keys assigned to the right hand are physically separated from the keys assigned to the left hand, often by several inches, to provide easier positions for the hands and arms.

If you learned to type with the correct fingers, you should have no problems with the division of the keyboard . If you learned "bad" habits such as reaching over for Ⓑ with your right forefinger, you'll need to unlearn such habits before you can use a split keyboard easily.

The Microsoft Natural Keyboard is perhaps the best known and most widely used split keyboard, but there are many others. More expensive and more ergonomic models, such as the Kinesis Advantage keyboard (shown in Figure A-1), use a well for each hand to put the fingers in a more comfortable typing position.

Split and Tilted Keyboards

Splitting the keys puts the hands and forearms into a more comfortable position, but both hands are still fully *pronated* (pointing downward). The next move on the ergonomic scale is to put the hands in a more neutral position by tilting the halves of the split keyboard away from each other. Various models of split and tilted keyboards are available, but one of the most popular is the Maxim keyboard (shown on the left

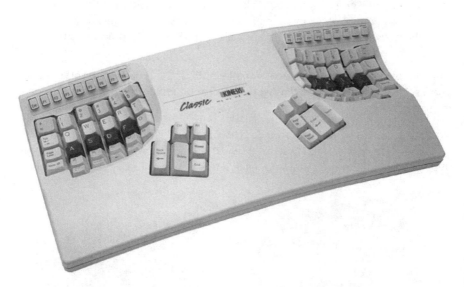

Figure A-1   *An example of a split keyboard: the Kinesis Advantage keyboard*

in Figure A-2) from Kinesis (**www.kinesis-ergo.com**). A more extreme split keyboard (and arguably a superergonomic keyboard) is the SafeType Ergonomic Keyboard (shown on the right in Figure A-2) from SafeType (**www.safetype.com**).

Superergonomic Keyboards

At this point, we move into the sphere of what you might term superergonomic keyboards. Here, things get either truly interesting or truly strange, depending on your perspective. This section presents samples of the types of keyboards you may want to examine if you need to improve your ergonomics beyond the point that split keyboards and split and tilted keyboards can deliver.

Superergonomic keyboards tackle the problem of repetitive keystrokes causing RSI in different ways: by using zero-force keys, by using different types of keys, or by not using keys at all.

FingerWorks TouchStream   The TouchStream keyboards from FingerWorks (**www.fingerworks.com**) include a custom pointing device that interprets the gestures from your hands. The TouchStream keyboards (Figure A-3 shows an example) are hard to comprehend without actually laying your hands on them and seeing what they do, but the combination of hardware and software is pretty amazing. For example, you click by tapping once with any two fingers together, and double-click by tapping once with any three fingers together. The keys themselves use what FingerWorks calls "zero-force"—you do press them, but with minimal force.

TouchStream keyboards are Mac compatible out of the box. FingerWorks even makes TouchStream models that work as a drop-in replacement for the keyboard on some models of PowerBook.

DataHand Ergonomic Keyboard   The DataHand Ergonomic Keyboard (Figure A-4) from DataHand Systems (**www.datahand.com**) is a radically different type of keyboard. In the DataHand, each finger occupies its own "well"—a hole

Figure A-2   *Split and tilted keyboards like the Maxim keyboard from Kinesis (left) and the SafeType Ergonomic Keyboard (right) from SafeType put the hands and forearms in a more neutral and comfortable position than flat keyboards.*

Figure A-3
The TouchStream keyboard from FingerWorks integrates mouse and gesture support in a zero-force keyboard.

that consists of five keys: a round button to press down (as in a standard typing motion), surrounded by four curved buttons, each of which you press outward. Each thumb controls six key switches, and the keyboard supports three modes, giving the equivalent of all the keys in a regular keyboard and more.

The DataHand is available in different hand sizes and costs from $975 to $1,275 at this writing, depending on whether you go for a personal model or a programmable professional model. Its cost puts the DataHand out of the reach of most consumers, but if your job involves huge amounts of data entry, and your company is forward-thinking enough to actively avoid repetitive stress injury problems, *and* you've been exercising your powers of persuasion, the DataHand might seem a viable choice.

orbiTouch Keyless Keyboard   The TouchStream and DataHand keyboards have different approaches to reducing the keypresses that cause repetitive-stress problems. But if pressing the keys is the problem, clearly the solution is to get rid of the keys altogether.

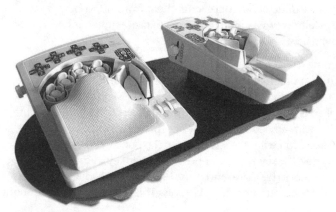

Figure A-4
The DataHand Ergonomic Keyboard is strange looking and expensive, but its devotees swear by it.

Choosing a Better Keyboard

Figure A-5
Instead of keys, the orbiTouch Keyless Keyboard has two domes, each of which you slide to any of eight positions.

You might think getting rid of the keys is a joke, but the orbiTouch Keyless Keyboard from Keybowl (**www.keybowl.com**) does just that. The orbiTouch (Figure A-5) is built around two domes that you move with your hands. Each of the domes slides to eight positions like the eight points of the compass. You type a letter by sliding the domes to the combination of their positions that represents that character. For example, to type a T, you slide the left dome to its North position and the right dome to its East position. To type an H, you slide the left dome to its East position and the right dome to its West position. The orbiTouch has an integrated mouse, so you can keep your hands on the domes the whole time.

One-Handed Keyboards

Last in our tour of specialized keyboards come one-handed keyboard models. There are two main types of one-handed keyboards: those designed to be used on the desktop or a similar stationary surface, and those designed to be held in the hand. Not surprisingly, given how most computers are used, the former category has more occupants than the latter.

Most one-handed desktop keyboards are designed for people suffering from a permanent or temporary disability that prevents them from using both hands. For example, P.C.D. Maltron (**www.maltron.com**) makes single-handed versions of its ergonomic keyboards.

The FrogPad (shown next) from the company of the same name (**www.frogpad .com**) is an ultracompact one-handed keyboard designed for right-handed use. FrogPad has a left-handed model in the works. Unlike the Maltron single-handed keyboards, the FrogPad is primarily intended for portable and wearable computers, although it works fine with any computer that accepts USB input. Because the FrogPad has only 20 keys, you enter the less used letters, punctuation, and symbols by *chording* (holding down a key while you press another key). For example, to enter an L, you hold down [Spacebar] and press [H]. The FrogPad also supports separate modes for entering numbers and symbols. The keyboard is well thought out and comfortable to use, but learning the letter positions and the chords takes considerable effort.

The Twiddler from Handykey is a handheld chording keyboard with a built-in pointing stick. The Twiddler works with either hand and connects to any computer that accepts Host USB, which makes it suitable for both desktop and handheld use. Strapped to your hand, the Twiddler feels very strange at first, and the learning curve feels precipitous. But if you put in the effort, you can get up to a decent typing speed (more than 50 words per minute) on a keyboard that you can use anywhere you have a hand free.

Page references to figures and illustrations are in italics.

INTERNATIONAL CONTACT INFORMATION

AUSTRALIA
McGraw-Hill Book Company
Australia Pty. Ltd.
TEL +61-2-9900-1800
FAX +61-2-9878-8881
http://www.mcgraw-hill.com.au
books-it_sydney@mcgraw-hill.com

CANADA
McGraw-Hill Ryerson Ltd.
TEL +905-430-5000
FAX +905-430-5020
http://www.mcgraw-hill.ca

GREECE, MIDDLE EAST, & AFRICA
(Excluding South Africa)
McGraw-Hill Hellas
TEL +30-210-6560-990
TEL +30-210-6560-993
TEL +30-210-6560-994
FAX +30-210-6545-525

MEXICO (Also serving Latin America)
McGraw-Hill Interamericana Editores
S.A. de C.V.
TEL +525-1500-5108
FAX +525-117-1589
http://www.mcgraw-hill.com.mx
carlos_ruiz@mcgraw-hill.com

SINGAPORE (Serving Asia)
McGraw-Hill Book Company
TEL +65-6863-1580
FAX +65-6862-3354
http://www.mcgraw-hill.com.sg
mghasia@mcgraw-hill.com

SOUTH AFRICA
McGraw-Hill South Africa
TEL +27-11-622-7512
FAX +27-11-622-9045
robyn_swanepoel@mcgraw-hill.com

SPAIN
McGraw-Hill/
Interamericana de España, S.A.U.
TEL +34-91-180-3000
FAX +34-91-372-8513
http://www.mcgraw-hill.es
professional@mcgraw-hill.es

UNITED KINGDOM, NORTHERN, EASTERN, & CENTRAL EUROPE
McGraw-Hill Education Europe
TEL +44-1-628-502500
FAX +44-1-628-770224
http://www.mcgraw-hill.co.uk
emea_queries@mcgraw-hill.com

ALL OTHER INQUIRIES Contact:
McGraw-Hill/Osborne
TEL +1-510-420-7700
FAX +1-510-420-7703
http://www.osborne.com
omg_international@mcgraw-hill.com